D1713096

CENSORSHIP AND INTELLECTUAL FREEDOM

A Survey of School Librarians' Attitudes and Moral Reasoning

by
FRANCES BECK McDONALD

The Scarecrow Press, Inc.
Metuchen, N.J., & London
1993

This book is based on the author's doctoral dissertation "Intellectual freedom and censorship attitudes of secondary school librarians and principal moral reasoning" for the University of Minnesota.

British Library Cataloguing-in-Publication data available

Library of Congress Cataloging-in-Publication Data

McDonald, Frances Beck, 1934-
    Censorship and intellectual freedom : a survey of school librarians' attitudes and moral reasoning / by Frances Beck McDonald.
        p.   cm.
    Based on the author's thesis (doctoral)—University of Minnesota. Includes bibliographical references (p.) and index.
    ISBN 0-8108-2680-1 (acid-free paper)
    1. School libraries—Censorship—United States—Public opinion. 2. School librarians—United States—Attitudes. 3. Moral development. 4. Judgment (Ethics) 5. Public opinion—United States. I. Title.
Z675.S3M327   1993
025.2'13—dc20   93-29500

For Intellectual Freedom Advocates,
who inspire and point the way.

For School Library Media Specialists,
who provide access and show the way.

CONTENTS

LIST OF TABLES

ACKNOWLEDGMENTS

Nothing we do is ever completely our own. Every project has roots in writings of others and contacts and conversations with many individuals. This project is no exception. I cannot name individuals, but I recognize and acknowledge their contributions.

While previous intellectual freedom and censorship research set the stage for this study, the work of two individuals specifically influenced the design of this research. Of note is the research conducted by Dr. Irene Getz on attitudes toward human rights and moral reasoning. Dr. Getz's study provided ideas for the methodology used in this study. Second, I especially acknowledge the 1971 study by Charles H. Busha on the attitudes of public librarians toward intellectual freedom and censorship. Dr. Busha's study provided the model for this study, including the methodology and development of the instrument to measure intellectual freedom and censorship attitudes.

I express thanks to the members of my thesis committee at the University of Minnesota where this project began. Dr. Howard Williams, my advisor, shared enthusiasm for freedom to read in schools. As a thesis advisor and teacher, Dr. Williams modeled respect for adult learners, allowed an individual to progress at her own pace, and provided constant positive encouragement and reinforcement. Dr. Norine Odland, a longtime defender of the right to read, provided helpful scholarly critique of the thesis.

Special thanks are due Dr. James Rest for the use of the *Defining Issues Test* and his calm, reassuring manner and helpful suggestions. My other committee members, Dr. Charles Bruning and Dr. John Stecklein, helped to make writing and defending a thesis a positive experience.

A debt of gratitude goes to the Iowa, Minnesota, and

Wisconsin school librarians who took time at the end of a school year to complete a rather lengthy questionnaire. Their assistance made this study possible.

Finally, I owe special thanks to my friend and editor, Dr. Dorothy Broderick. For many in our profession, Dorothy represents the model of an intellectual freedom advocate. I am no exception. In addition, my introduction to the Kohlberg theory of moral development came from "Moral Values and Children's Literature," a chapter in Dorothy's book, *Issues in Children's Book Selection.* While the thesis was in progress she provided much needed prodding, and after its completion, suggested this publication. Most important, Dorothy's editorial suggestions helped to transform a thesis into something readable.

While I acknowledge and thank all who contributed to this work, I take responsibility for errors of thought, design, or interpretation.

FOREWORD

The library profession has an all-consuming interest in censorship and intellectual freedom issues. We collect articles and create files about censorship, we monitor incidents of censorship, and make lists of censored titles. In our writing and speaking, we speculate about reasons for challenges and censorship. We know the details of censorship incidents, but the motivation of major players in the scenarios remains a mystery. We have many opinions, but little hard data. The search for data to verify our speculations leads a few of us to conduct research.

This study raises awareness of the gap between professional beliefs and practices. Perhaps the library profession did not need another study showing that librarians demonstrate conflicts between their attitudes toward the principles of their profession and applying the principles. Perhaps we did not need to hear another time that not all librarians agree with the values of their profession. However, becoming aware of a discrepancy between values and behavior is the first step toward adopting and acting on values. For some readers, it might be the beginning of the process leading to acting on professional values.

Combining the results reported here with results reported in other studies appears to validate one conclusion. Level of education is emerging as a significant variable in explaining attitudes toward intellectual freedom and censorship. It is to be hoped that library educators will take seriously the challenges offered by these results. The information that success in teaching the principles of our profession is not matched by success in teaching how to apply the principles has implications for library educators. The curriculum and teaching and learning strategies need to be examined. Library educators in programs not accredited by the American

Library Association apparently must give more attention to teaching the principles of the profession. For state licensing agencies and policymakers influencing the certification of school librarians, these results provide another reason for giving serious consideration to the *Information Power* recommendation that the master's degree be established as the entry level degree for school library professionals.

As with much of research in librarianship, censorship, and intellectual freedom research is long on counting but short on explaining. Descriptive research studies tell us what is, but do not help us to understand why. This study also tells what is, but also stops short of providing reasons why. The next stage of research, long overdue, should explore beyond a description of the characteristics of librarians and their attitudes to influences on behavior and reasons for behavior. Researchers need to examine all stages of motivation in upholding the principles of our profession.

This publication has several purposes. For the researcher, the affirmation of findings in previous studies about intellectual freedom and censorship attitudes provides a stepping stone for the next stage of research. For the library educator, the findings provide a challenge to examine teaching methods and curriculum. For the practitioner, the findings offer a chance to compare personal professional values and beliefs with those collectively reported here.

Protection of access to information occurs school by school, incident by incident, when each school librarian applies the principles of the profession without compromise. If access to information is not protected for each student in every school, it makes no difference what findings are reported, what descriptions are offered, what profiles of librarians are constructed with data from statistical studies. It is audacious to think that one publication could influence the behavior of librarians, but it is irresponsible and contrary to the philosophy of an educator not to try. If access to information is an important professional value, and I believe it is, and if this publication reminds one school librarian of the responsibility to act on professional values, thus contributing to protecting access to information, then the purposes will have been met.

FRANCES BECK MCDONALD, PH.D.
Library Media Education
Mankato State University
Mankato, Minnesota 56002

CHAPTER 1
INTELLECTUAL FREEDOM:
A PROFESSIONAL VALUE

The library profession proudly claims freedom to read and freedom of access to information as preeminent values. Librarians endorse protection of freedom to read in their "Code of Ethics" and consider dissemination of information a basic professional responsibility. Librarians react with collective indignation when resources are challenged by citizens or removed by government authorities.

The principles of intellectual freedom and unrestricted access to information are based in the First Amendment of the Bill of Rights of the Constitution of the United States. The "Library Bill of Rights" and "Freedom to Read" documents endorsed by the library community represent the translation of freedom of speech into library practice.

Two hundred years after the adoption of the Bill of Rights, rather than being an accepted national value, the First Amendment continues to be attacked. Within the past decade, self-appointed protectors of the public morals have attacked record albums, live performances, and respected museum photographic exhibits. Around the country pornography is attacked under the guise of protecting women from violence. Access to government information is restricted for economic reasons or ostensibly to protect national security. Controversy occurs over the teaching of scientific theories. Classroom resources are challenged and library collections scrutinized for books that critics consider harmful to children.

First Amendment restrictions occur in schools to protect children, to maintain civility, to protect the sensibilities of members of minority groups, to deny the Holocaust, to maintain respect for authority, and to limit textbook content to that which presents patriotic and positive accounts of our history. While some of the onslaught against the First Amendment stems from deeply held religious beliefs, other attempts to restrict access stem from concerned parents trying to protect their children from unpleasant depictions of human behavior. These parents seek a verbal and visual world in which nothing will be scary, nothing will be silly, nothing will be unpleasant, and nothing will be real. They rally to remove resources they view as threatening to the cocoon in which they wish to raise their children.

Not all efforts to restrict access to information and ideas in schools come from religious groups or parents, however. School administrators, school boards, and teachers initiate restrictions, often with success, because of their positions within the school.

Librarians are not immune from being influenced by attempts to restrict access. Nor do all librarians react the same way to restrictions and challenges. A restrictive social climate gives some librarians permission to exercise their instinct to restrict resources in media centers. Faced with requests to remove resources from school administrators and teachers, some librarians, without hesitation, remove them. Other librarians, when ordered to remove titles, would like to resist, but are unwilling to risk trouble by challenging the order. Librarians remove resources because they find it more expedient to acquiesce to the wishes of their superiors and colleagues than to exercise professional responsibility. Yet there are librarians who see no reason why restrictions outside the school should affect their access decisions in the school. These librarians resist efforts to restrict and successfully convince colleagues of the value of providing diverse resources to meet the needs of students and teachers.

Unwilling to admit being censors, members of the library community deny that their decisions about access to resources constitute censorship situations. Or, admitting restrictive behavior, librarians justify the restrictions as responding to the wishes of the community, or as being of little harm. When Cal Thomas (1983) challenged the library community to prove that their practices were not so censorious as efforts to restrict originating from the conservative community, librarians were indignant. Few librarians have ever had to publicly acknowledge that their practices were censorship. A historical perspective provides some insight into how librarians viewed censorious behavior in the past.

INTELLECTUAL FREEDOM AND LIBRARIANS: HISTORICAL PERSPECTIVE

The library community has not always viewed protection of freedom to read as one of its responsibilities. Librarianship as a profession in the United States had its beginnings in 1876, the year the American Library Association was organized. In 1876, operating under the national climate of the Comstock Law of 1873, principles of freedom to read were not part of the professional ethic. Librarians avoided controversial literature and endorsed themselves as moral censors. Libraries were established to promote literacy and religion, to become the people's university, and to provide activities for workers during their leisure hours, but not to provide unrestricted access to information. Early libraries were not available to children or women and operated under strict rules of circulation.

The singular study tracing the changing role of the librarian as censor to the librarian as protector of freedom to read was published in 1984. Geller (1984:13) described the motivation of the librarian during the late nineteenth and early twentieth centuries. "The intent of exclusion was not opinion control but the affirmation of religious and political freedom and, more, of tolerance. In that era, when extreme statements of extreme views circulated in abundance, the library promised noninterference with cherished social identities." Moral censorship was assumed and librarians considered themselves guardians of the public taste. "Censorship crystallized as a symbol of the librarian's role, autonomy, and guiding function" (Geller 1984: 13, 79).

Before and during World War I, the role of the librarian as moral censor continued, and librarians expanded their censorship role by identifying and limiting access to unpopular political literature. But, during this same time, librarians began to question the idea of the librarian as censor. Some librarians looked to the First Amendment for a rationale for their changing ideology.

> In World War I, a deepening and ugly intolerance spread to attacks on library collections. . . . Many librarians acquiesced willingly, even eagerly, in this patriotic zeal. Putting the role of citizen above that of the professional, putting advocacy above their traditional neutrality, they happily censored their libraries and helped prepare lists of prohibited books. Others, however, to protect their collections, began to develop an ideology of freedom, resorting, for the first time, to First Amendment principles. Ironically, the defense of freedom itself cast into relief the rules of censorship that governed library service, norms that were not yet questioned. (Geller 1984: 109)

The idea of the library as an institution existing for the defense of freedom to read continued to appear in professional literature following World War I. Library practices, however, lagged behind the ideology. Defending freedom to read was limited by the recognition that self-censorship as part of the librarian's expertise was expected.

> The library profession began to act as an interest group in defense of a limited freedom. As new strategies of defense were developed, the value of freedom came to replace censorship, and to supplement neutrality, in defining professional and social responsibility. (Geller 1984: 127)
>
> Most defenses of freedom, nevertheless, were limited, containing the implication that a judicious self-censorship was expected as part of the librarian's expertise in judging books and in assessing local community standards. (Geller 1984: 136)

Since 1939, the "Library Bill of Rights" has guided the actions of librarians and an ethic of freedom to read rather than censorship has permeated the profession. In 1939, the profession approved a "Library Bill of Rights," modeled on one developed in 1938 by Forrest Spaulding of the Des Moines Public Library. The move to approve the "Library Bill of

Rights" originated, not with library leaders devoted to preserving the status quo, but with grass-roots librarians putting pressure on their library leaders. At that time, Archibald MacLeish, the poet named Librarian of Congress, addressed librarians and underscored the role of the librarian in a democracy. "If [librarians] saw themselves as selecting from the record the books that people needed for their decisions, they could, in this 'impending democratic crisis,' validate a way of government and a way of life" (Geller 1984: 159, 179).

In the century following the founding of the profession, librarians moved from a position of moral censorship as part of their professional responsibility to their patrons to one of defense of freedom to read as their professional responsibility to library users. In spite of strong verbal acceptance of the principles stated in the "Library Bill of Rights," however, librarians differ widely in professional practices assuring unrestricted access to information in libraries. In spite of belonging to a profession that advocates strong "freedom to read" principles, librarians censor and librarians hold differing beliefs about restrictions on access to information.

VOLUNTARY CENSORSHIP

Censorship of educational resources is a major concern for school librarians and other educators. Discussions about censorship have focused on demands from organized groups and parents to remove materials from schools. Attention has also been given to the role of the school board and school administrators in determining what will be allowed to remain on the shelves of school libraries. Less attention has been given to voluntary censorship performed by librarians. Voluntary censorship occurs when the librarian, as a result of real or anticipated pressures from school personnel or persons in the community, removes or restricts resources, or does not purchase certain titles.

A few writers have tried to identify the characteristics of censorious librarians. Downs (1984: 8) suggested that perhaps something in the psychological makeup or personality of librarians accounted for their differing approaches to the selection and restriction of library resources. Fiske (1959: 110) concluded that librarians do not feel strongly enough "as individuals or professionals" to assert intellectual freedom values in the "face of public disapproval." Busha (1972) asked whether there were personality traits associated with attitudes toward censorship and found a significant correlation between authoritarian beliefs and tendency to censor. These observations and questions about why librarians differ in their commitment to professional beliefs led to this study.

Perhaps school librarians holding different attitudes toward intellectual freedom and censorship also exhibit different personal characteristics, such as level of ego development, conceptual level, and level of moral development. Because of the close relationship between moral judgments about justice and values and decisions about providing equal access to resources, level of moral reasoning of librarians offered a characteristic to examine as part of the explanation for differing attitudes. This study was designed to explore the relationship between the attitudes of secondary school librarians toward intellectual freedom and censorship and selected demographic variables and one additional characteristic: level of principled moral reasoning.

REFERENCES

Busha, Charles H. *Freedom Versus Suppression and Censorship: With a Study of the Attitudes of Midwestern Public Librarians and a Bibliography of Censorship*. Littleton, Colorado: Libraries Unlimited, 1972.

Downs, Robert B., and Ralph E. McCoy, eds. *The First Freedom Today: Critical Issues Relating to Censorship and Intellectual Freedom*. Chicago: American Library Association, 1984.

Fiske, Marjorie (Lowenthal). *Book Selection and Censorship: A Study of School and Public Librarians in California*. Berkeley: University of California Press, 1959.

Geller, Evelyn. *Forbidden Books in American Public Libraries, 1876–1939: A Study in Cultural Change*. Westport, Connecticut: Greenwood Press, 1984.

Thomas, Cal. *Book Burning*. Westchester, Illinois: Crossways Books, Good News Publishers, 1983.

CHAPTER 2
INTELLECTUAL FREEDOM AND CENSORSHIP: RELATED LITERATURE

The library profession espouses equal access to information for all patrons in all libraries. One document, the "Library Bill of Rights," stands as the singular statement guiding librarians in their application of the principles of intellectual freedom in libraries. Based upon the guarantee of free speech in the First Amendment to the United States Constitution, the "Library Bill of Rights" addresses issues of access, criteria for selection, and the proactive stance to be taken by librarians in defense of freedom-to-read principles. Interpretations of the "Library Bill of Rights" provide further guidance to librarians applying intellectual freedom principles in libraries.

The "Library Bill of Rights" applies to all types of libraries, including school libraries, as indicated in the statement, "Books and other library resources should be provided for the interest, information, and enlightenment of all people of the community the library serves." From 1955 until 1976, the American Association of School Librarians endorsed a separate document known as the "School Library Bill of Rights." This document stated that "the American Association of School Librarians reaffirms its belief in the 'Library Bill of Rights' of the American Library Association" and continued with a description of the responsibilities of the school librarian. The two documents presented a source of confusion both within and outside the library community. When a 1967 revision of the "Library Bill of Rights" added opposition to information restrictions because of age, the " 'School Library Bill of Rights' became largely redundant." However, the Board of Directors of the American Association of School Librarians did not withdraw the "School Library Bill of

Rights" until 1976 (American Library Association 1989). Continued requests for a statement related specifically to school libraries resulted in a document titled "Access to Resources and Services in the School Library Media Program: An Interpretation of the Library Bill of Rights," adopted in 1986. These two statements—the "Library Bill of Rights" and the interpretation, "Access to Resources and Services in the School Library Media Program"—provide professional guidance to school librarians applying intellectual freedom principles in school libraries. (Copies of the documents are provided in Appendix A.)

SCHOOL LIBRARY STANDARDS

National standards for school library media programs provide further evidence of the commitment of school librarians to the concepts of intellectual freedom held by the library profession. The 1960 Standards listed a basic principle for the selection of materials.

> Administrators, classroom and special teachers, and the library staff endorse and apply the principles incorporated in the "School Library Bill of Rights" of the American Association of School Librarians, and in any statements for the selection of library materials that school librarians have helped to formulate for the state or for the local school system. (American Library Association 1960: 74)

In 1969, revised Standards (American Library Association 1969: 20) affirmed as basic policy "such American freedoms as described in the 'Library Bill of Rights,' [and] the 'School Library Bill of Rights.'" Added to this endorsement was a recommendation that schools "have a written statement of selection policy, formulated and endorsed by the school administration, the media specialists, and faculty, and adopted by the school board." The 1975 Standards, *Media Programs: District and School* (American Library Association 1975: 64) again affirmed the need for a selection policy which "reflects and supports principles of intellectual freedom described in the 'Library Bill of Rights,' the 'School Library Bill of Rights,' and 'The Student's Right to Read.' " The latest national guidelines, *Information Power: Guidelines for School Library Media Programs* (1988) point out that the mission of the school library requires "the serious commitment . . . to the value of universal and unrestricted access to information and ideas."

The importance of following the principles of intellectual freedom is described in the profession's "Code of Ethics." Adopted by the American Library Association in 1981, the "Code of Ethics" affirms that

> librarians significantly influence or control the selection, organization, preservation, and dissemination of information. In a political system grounded in an informed citizenry, librarians are members of a profession explicitly committed to intellectual freedom and the freedom of access to information. We have a special obligation to ensure the free flow of information and ideas to present and future generations. . . . Librarians must resist all efforts by groups or individuals to censor library materials.

(The "Code of Ethics" is reprinted in Appendix A.)

Censorship Research

Most research about censorship in schools and libraries reports challenges to library resources: how many incidents, who initiated the challenges, and the results of the challenges. The National Coalition Against Censorship monitors censorship controversies in school systems around the country and operates a clearinghouse of information about censorship incidents that reach the courts. Although there were virtually no school library censorship cases before the early 1970s, there are court decisions now. Based on a summary of recent court cases, the National Coalition Against Censorship concluded,

No idea is immune from attack. Books, films and
magazines *spanning* a broad range of content have been
challenged. Nor is any *place* spared: court cases arise in
many different parts of the country, in both metropolitan and rural areas, in classrooms and in school libraries,
and in elementary, junior and senior high schools.
(National Coalition Against Censorship 1985: 4)

The longest series of studies of censorship in schools was
conducted by Burress of the Wisconsin Council of Teachers
of English and the National Council of Teachers of English.
From 1963 when the results of the first Wisconsin survey
were published, the practice of self-censorship was evident.
"There is much self-censorship. How much, it is difficult to
measure, but many of the reports indicated explicit or implicit
censorship." Restrictive activities included removing controversial books from the collection and discarding them, or
placing potentially controversial titles in collections reserved
for teacher use or on shelves restricted to certain students, or
refusing to purchase certain titles because of the suspected
controversial nature of the book or because of the librarian's
personal opinions (Burress 1984: 1–32).

The second Burress study, completed in 1973, included a
national sample as well as the sample from Wisconsin schools.
Burress found that 28 percent of the national sample and 26
percent of the Wisconsin sample reported objections to
resources used in schools. These percentages were up from
the 22 percent reporting objections in 1963. Again, Burress
found that almost half of the objections originated from
school staff (Burress 1984: 60–101).

In 1983, Burress reported the results of his most recent
national survey. Burress found that more than 50 percent of
the responding librarians had experienced challenges to
resources. While Burress acknowledged a "high degree of
fear or uncertainty" among the school librarians, he also
suggested that librarians appeared more willing than teachers
to defend the First Amendment (Burress 1983).

From an analysis of censorship incidents reported in the
Newsletter on Intellectual Freedom, Woods (1979) reported that
school administrators and teachers initiated most of the

censorship attempts within the schools. Woods pointed out, however, that school librarians were unlikely to report self-censorship or prior censorship to the publication of an association that strongly advocates principles of intellectual freedom.

More than one in five librarians reported challenges to resources in schools in a nationwide study designed to measure rates of censorship from 1978 to 1980. One in four of the respondents indicated that the rate of challenge had increased over the previous two-year period. Challenges were reported by librarians in all areas of the country and in all sizes of communities. Responses revealed that individuals, mostly parents, initiated the challenges in three-fourths of the cases. Resources were removed, restricted or altered in half the cases (Association of American Publishers, 1981).

During the 1980s, beginning with the Minnesota Civil Liberties Union 1983 survey, several state Civil Liberties Union studies were conducted. Thirty-seven percent of the responding secondary school librarians in Minnesota reported challenges to school library materials. Thirty-six percent of these challenges resulted in the removal or restriction of the resource questioned (McDonald 1983). Similar studies were conducted in Nebraska and North Carolina. A four-state American Civil Liberties Union study published in 1985 reported censorship in Georgia, Tennessee, Louisiana, and Alabama. "Several respondents indicated that self-censorship may be widespread" (National Commission on Libraries and Information Science 1986: 29).

Censorship and Librarians

The landmark study of the role of the librarian in the selection, removal, restriction, or retention of resources in schools and public libraries was reported in 1959. Investigating California librarians, Fiske found that belief in the concepts of intellectual freedom did not always translate into actual selection practices. California school and public librarians did not always follow the tenets of intellectual freedom in their initial selection of resources, nor did the principles of intellectual freedom necessarily guide the librarians' responses to attempts to remove or restrict resources. Nearly one-half of the librarians interviewed expressed strong agreement with intellectual freedom principles, but two-thirds reported instances when the controversial nature of a book or author resulted in a decision not to purchase the item.

Based on extensive interviews with librarians in twenty-six California communities, Fiske observed that "many restrictive practices have been spontaneously incorporated into the routine procedures of both public and school libraries without any apparent external cause" (1959: 2). The primary question of the Fiske study was "whether restrictions are being imposed on librarians, or whether they are imposing restrictions on themselves, that threaten the citizen's right to easy access to as adequate a collection of books and periodicals as his community, his county or his state can afford" (Fiske 1959: viii).

Fiske found that librarians resisted 56 percent of the complaints from outside their institutions, but 85 percent of the materials questioned from within were removed or restricted. "Books complained about by patrons or others outside the institution were by no means as likely to result in restrictions or removals as were those questioned by librarians themselves or by others within their institutions" (Fiske 1959: 70). Furthermore, Fiske found little indication that librarians opposed removal of materials by teachers or administrators.

Fiske (1959: 110–111) concluded that "librarians do not feel strong enough as individuals or professionals to assert [intellectual freedom values] in the face of public disapproval or indifference." Recognizing the conflict between their practices and their professional responsibilities, librarians criticized themselves for being "too prone to compromise" and "too cautious or too evasive." Fiske (1959: 47–48) found that librarians took one of three approaches to complaints: adopted a "philosophical" or "long-suffering" stance, initiated restrictive measures, or made certain that there was nothing in the collection for anyone to complain about.

Following the Fiske research, but investigating only school librarians, Farley (1964) made a distinction between involuntary censorship, that which occurred because of pressures on the librarian, and voluntary censorship, that performed by a librarian because of personal convictions. Farley (1964: 116–117) concluded that all librarians performed some voluntary censorship and cited reasons related to two factors:

> the belief that reading can have some kind of undesirable or corruptive effect upon character, personality, or conduct, and the belief that the users of the high school library are too young, too immature, and unprepared to cope with some ideas, facts, opinions, or depictions of life that are to be found in books.

Farley conducted extensive interviews with one librarian in each of fifty-four high school libraries in Nassau County, New York. A large number of librarians being interviewed avoided using the term "censor" and insisted that they were not censors although at some point in each interview, the librarians stated that they "usually" or "sometimes did" or "probably would" censor. To these librarians, censors were those who exerted pressure from outside the school. Librarians appeared not to see that decisions they made were censorship. Eleven percent of the librarians in Nassau County exhibited clearly restrictive attitudes. Thirty-three percent of the librarians were permissive, and 55.5 percent of the librarians were described as "wavering or weak," that is, neither clearly restrictive nor strongly in favor of freedom of access to books. Restrictive librarians made statements "that showed that they favored a rather large amount of book censorship in the high school library, or that there was a rather wide range of allegedly controversial subjects which they believed should be excluded from a library used by young people" (Farley 1964: 122).

In terms of behavior, Farley (1964: 122) found that 9.2 percent of the librarians habitually censored materials and 61.1 percent sometimes avoided controversial books. The controversial nature of a book did not influence selection for 29.6 percent of the librarians. Librarians classified as favoring freedom of access, while not saying that high school students could read anything they pleased, made statements "that could be classified as favoring a wide latitude of permissiveness in reading by adolescents, or made statements strongly in favor of the freedom of young people to read without many restrictions, or against any but the minimum of censorship."

Busha (1972) examined Midwestern public librarians to determine their attitudes toward intellectual freedom, censorship, and authoritarian beliefs. Busha found that Midwestern public librarians professed strong intellectual freedom beliefs, but he also found that Midwestern public librarians showed "a marked disparity between [their] attitudes toward intellectual freedom as a concept and their attitudes toward censorship as an activity."

Using language from the "Library Bill of Rights" and the "Freedom to Read" statement, Busha constructed a scale designed to measure agreement with intellectual freedom principles. The measure of censorship attitudes was constructed with agree/disagree statements describing library practices that would indicate a restrictive attitude toward patron access to resources. As Fiske had in the 1950s, Busha found a fairly high and statistically significant correlation between intellectual freedom and censorship scores. Librarians who agreed with intellectual freedom disapproved of censorship, although not in direct proportion to the degree of approval of intellectual freedom principles. Busha also found a statistically significant correlation of .73 between censorship and authoritarianism. Librarians who agreed with authoritarian beliefs also tended to agree with censorship measures at an application level. "It is evident that Midwestern public librarians did not hesitate to express agreement with cliches of intellectual freedom but that many of them apparently did not feel strongly enough about them as professionals to assert these principles in the face of real or anticipated censorship pressures" (Busha 1971: 151).

Investigating the intellectual freedom and censorship attitudes of public librarians in six Ontario cities, England (1974) found that librarians "were not strong proponents of intellectual freedom, and their willingness to agree with the concept of intellectual freedom only slightly exceeded their willingness to be liberal and non-censorious." Personal views of these public librarians and their perceptions of the views of others were found to influence collections more than the librarians' views of intellectual freedom.

Bump (1980) investigated librarians in 608 North Central Association accredited high schools in west central states to determine how much the controversial nature of a book influenced the selection activities of librarians. Bump's checklist of controversial titles included twenty-five titles that had received four or more censorship attempts between 1965 and 1979 as reported in the *Newsletter on Intellectual Freedom*. Contrary to other reported research, Bump found that librarians were not influenced by censorship incidents elsewhere when books were already in the collection. Further, the librarians used criteria other than potential censorship to determine what materials would be selected. Specifically, these librarians considered how the book fit into their collections. However, Bump also found evidence that librarians were not likely to select books that offended them personally. Librarians in the study were "considered professionally competent by their administrators and [were] not generally subjected to an administrative censorship process before books [were] ordered" (Bump 1980: 136).

Ninety-four percent of the public librarians surveyed by Bundy and Stakem (1982: 585) agreed that "a chief commitment of a professional librarian should be to intellectual freedom for everyone." But as Fiske had previously, these researchers found that librarians' personal opinions at times influenced what resources were made available to their clients and that there might be some types of materials that librarians would restrict. While their study did not prove bias in collection building and reference, the authors stated that they believed it existed. Based on their findings, Bundy and Stakem (1982: 589) suggested that

> many librarians do not have a consistent philosophical base to their views on intellectual freedom. Without this base, class and race and personal views on such subjects as homosexuality can too readily influence buying and reference decisions. . . . We believe that whether from naivete or design, the stance of neutrality also results in

keeping out opinions and views that librarians do not themselves approve.

Write-in comments by respondents to a national study of censorship sponsored by the Association of American Publishers, the American Library Association, and the Association for Supervision and Curriculum Development (1981: 12) provided "evidence that the difficult-to-document phenomenon of precensorship does occur in our schools." Librarians responding to this survey named school personnel as initiating more than 30 percent of the challenges to resources in public schools. Librarians avoided selecting controversial materials for school library media centers, not because the materials did not meet educational criteria, but because the materials did "not conform to the personal values of the individuals making selection."

That librarians do not view their actions as censorship was also evident in responses to the Minnesota Civil Liberties Union survey. No responding librarian reported initiating a challenge, although comments indicated that secondary school librarians indeed censored materials, either at the point of purchase, or at the request of other school personnel. The comments offered by two librarians illustrate typical explanations for censorious behavior: "I have had two different principals order me to remove ——— and I removed them" or "the superintendent has expressed that I keep the community in mind with book ordering" (McDonald 1983: 10).

Jenkinson (1979) studied the tactics of more than two hundred organizations whose purposes were to monitor resources used in schools. The actions of these groups frequently resulted in attempts to have books and other resources removed from classrooms and libraries. Although focusing on the work of these citizens in classrooms, Jenkinson pointed out that "individuals and groups know that they do not have to be in positions of authority to have books banned from the public schools; rather, they know that in some school systems they simply need to exert sufficient pressure on school boards, school administrators, and/or classroom teachers to realize their goal." This resulted in what Jenkinson called "closet censorship," which occurred when teachers or librarians decided not to purchase an item, or quietly withdrew titles that were the object of controversy elsewhere.

> When a teacher reads that *The Catcher in the Rye,* for example, is being protested in a nearby community, he or she may decide not to teach that book again in fear of censorship. That is closet censorship. When a librarian fails to order a book because it has provoked criticism from irate taxpayers in other communities, that is closet censorship. When a department chairperson locks up all copies of John Steinbeck's *Of Mice and Men* because one parent quietly objected to the book, that's closet censorship. And when a teacher takes a felt-tip pen and marks out a word in all copies of an anthology, that's closet censorship. (Jenkinson 1979)

Jenkinson suggested that these are examples of hundreds of incidents that are never reported. Such actions are performed without anyone knowing about them, since the teachers or librarians involved typically do not report the incidents to the press or school authorities.

In a 1965 study of secondary teachers of English, Ahrens found that there was "a good deal of internal censorship by school and library personnel that eliminated books before they ever reached the hand of the student reader" (Ahrens 1965: 19). Although finding censorship incidents reported by only 12 percent of her respondents, Ahrens concluded that the publicity surrounding the incidents led to self-censorship elsewhere.

> That the censorship incidents for the most part were relatively quiet, undramatic events is made clear in these data. The bomb threats, mass meetings, even newspaper reports were few in number. Unfortunately, however, it is the latter kind of incident which—because of widespread publicity—can trigger events in other areas, or cause an increase in "caution" and pre-censorship by teachers. (Ahrens 1965: 92)

Douma (1976: 64) observed that objections from librarians and teachers resulted in the removal of books from libraries more often than objections from parents. In a review of censorship studies, Douma concluded that voluntary censorship occurred most often in relationship to materials about sex, sectarian books, art books with nudes, and "extreme one-sided treatment of communism or race." Douma reasoned that such self-censorship resulted from the "librarian's belief that some kinds of reading can have ill effects upon the character and conduct of readers" and that children were especially vulnerable because of their immaturity.

Flagg (1986) surveyed seventy-eight secondary school librarians in Missouri about periodical purchases for the school library. She found that 63 percent would be influenced by complaints from community or faculty members, 72 percent by administrators, and 64 percent by complaints coming from parents. Flagg concluded, however, that "data indicated that Missouri librarians may indeed be assuming roles of 'gatekeeper' in that they tended to either not order periodicals or cancel subscriptions more frequently because of their own objections than those of the administration, students, teachers, or parents."

Hopkins (1984: 9–22) surveyed perceptions of censorship held by state education agency school library media supervisors and professional youth library association leaders. The most frequently voiced concern by both groups was their perception of a trend toward self-censorship by school library media specialists. These leaders suggested that a climate of fear caused self-censorship of controversial materials. They also pointed out that decreases in funding might be used as an excuse not to purchase certain items. Even the Supreme Court decision in *Pico* (1982), according to Hopkins, could have the effect of encouraging self-censorship.

> Precensorship might actually be encouraged by school board officials and school administrators. While they may be less likely to remove materials, they may be more likely to precensor materials before they are purchased. (Hopkins 1984: 19)

There are two stages when censorship practices are likely to be exhibited by librarians: at the point of selection and at the point of access. Twenty-nine percent of Fiske's school librarians were conscious of controversy at the point of selection (1959: 66). She found that 20 percent of the school librarians she interviewed habitually avoided buying controversial or potentially controversial materials, and almost 60 percent reported instances where the controversial nature of a book or author resulted in a decision not to buy. Even among those librarians who held strong freedom-to-read convictions, controversiality of a book was taken into account, especially if a more legitimate reason could also be found to avoid purchasing a book. Reasons providing legitimacy included identification of a title as "trash" or of a "too advanced reading level" (Fiske 1959: 65, 125).

Pope (1974) studied the opinions of school, public, and academic librarians about sexually oriented literature. He used institutional, professional, and personal characteristics such as age, sex, and marital status to analyze the results of his research. Based on an assumption that sexually oriented literature had the most likelihood of being considered controversial, Pope (1974: 183) investigated the opinions of school, public, and academic librarians about selecting this type of literature for their respective libraries. While all the librarians surveyed identified some types of sex literature that they would not select, school librarians were more restrictive than other types of librarians. Rejection rates ran as high as 81.9 percent for school librarians, compared with 47.6 percent for public librarians and 31.0 percent for academic librarians.

Pressures encouraging self-censorship come from within the profession as well as from administrators and the outside. Wondering about the practice of a library jobber putting a warning signal—a pink slip—in books that had received complaints about objectionable content, Watson and Snider (1981: 95–101) designed a study to examine the influence of warning symbols on selection. Watson and Snider found that, in spite of favorably written reviews, "adult book selectors reject to a great extent children's books based on reviews identified by a warning symbol." This finding led the researchers to conclude that warning symbols encouraged the "most insidious form of censorship," that of self-censorship. Watson and Snider (1981: 99) suggested that

> professional children's book reviewers, trusted for their assumed objective and critical analysis skills, might identify and denounce objectionable content only when such objectionable elements are judged to be blatantly, excessively, and exploitively used in a shocking and startlingly distasteful style.

Woodworth (1976) surveyed librarians, teachers, and administrators in Wisconsin and concluded that self-censorship was evident.

> If a librarian objects to a library book chances are he/she will not select it for purchase, will restrict access to it, or will remove it after a problem has surfaced. These matters are rarely reported directly, but surface through comments on selecting for the conservative nature of the community, and the like. (1976: 59)

The attitudes of the librarians in Woodworth's study also indicated less than full commitment to intellectual freedom. Fifty-four percent of the librarians surveyed agreed or strongly agreed with the statement, "No society nor school can operate without some censorship." Further, 13 percent of the librarians disagreed or strongly disagreed with the statement, "Censorship is a violation of our freedom of expression guaranteed by the Bill of Rights."

Variables Related to Censorship

Based on her review of censorship literature, Serebnick (1979) identified six variables that could influence the selection and censorship activities of librarians. Serebnick pointed out that most research had focused on librarian variables, specifically restrictiveness resulting from attitudes, age, and educational attainment, among other factors. She attributed this research focus to the Fiske study (1959), which centered on the librarian as censor and to the fact that it is the librarian

Table 1

Selection and Censorship Variables in Libraries

Class I. LIBRARIAN VARIABLES

    a. Librarians' Attitudes Toward Censorship and Intellectual Freedom
    b. Demographic Variables (for example, age, education)
    c. Perceived Role of Library and Librarians in the Community

Class II. LIBRARY VARIABLES

    a. Organizational, Administrative, and Legal Structure of the Library
    b. Selection Policies
    c. Budget

Class III. COMMUNITY LEADER VARIABLES

    a. Community Leaders' Attitudes Toward Censorship and Intellectual Freedom
    b. Community Leaders' Interest in and Influence over the Library

Class IV. COMMUNITY AND COMMUNITY ACTION VARIABLES

    a. Census Data (for example, size and density of populations served, educational levels)
    b. Pressure Groups in the Community
    c. Nature, Number, and Resolution of Censorial Actions in the Community

Class V. MASS MEDIA VARIABLES

    a. Coverage of Censorship and Intellectual Freedom in Mass Media (for example, book review media, newspapers)
    b. Relationship of Mass Media to the Library (for example, which book review journals are read)

Class VI. JUDICIAL AND LEGAL VARIABLES

    a. Judicial Decisions Regarding Censorship and Intellectual Freedom
    b. Federal, State, and Local Legislation Regarding Censorship and Intellectual Freedom

Source: Serebnick, Judith. *Collection Building* 1 (1979), 13–15.

who selects materials, Serebnick suggested however, that research is needed on all classes of variables.

Downs identified four public institutions that have traditionally ignored the Bill of Rights—the military, the schools, mental hospitals, and prisons. Downs asserted,

> First Amendment rights are severely restricted and often prohibited in all four. They deny the right of free trial to persons accused of misconduct, and consider authority more important than freedom, order more precious than liberty, and discipline more valuable than individual expression. Military commanders, school principals, chief psychiatrists, and prison wardens, it is suggested, have similar characteristics in the governance of their respective organizations. (Downs 1984: 23)

That the attitudes and expectations of a school principal influence school librarians was demonstrated by Fiske (1959: 31, 86, 98) who found that librarians working for restrictive administrators tended to be restrictive, regardless of community pressures or lack of them. Fiske also found that librarians who worked with principals who supported freedom to read tended also to support the freedom to read. "Staff members . . . tend to reflect their superiors' attitudes."

From an analysis of research based on checklists, Serebnick (1982) observed that some of the conclusions offered by researchers provided insights into the collection development process employed by librarians. But she expressed caution about using evidence from checklist-based research to conclude that librarians practiced self-censorship. Serebnick criticized checklist-based research because some of the studies lacked standardized definitions of censorship and self-censorship, and some lacked criteria for inclusion of titles on lists. Serebnick suggested that factors other than self-censorship by librarians might account for the fact that titles listed in a checklist were not included in a specific library collection.

Serebnick (1981) found no evidence of self-censorship

among the New Jersey public librarians she investigated. Choosing mass media as the variable to investigate, Serebnick focused on the book reviews librarians typically use when selecting books. She identified six reviewing journals used by librarians. Serebnick found a significant positive correlation (.69) between the number of reviews a book received and the likelihood of the title being found in a public library, but did not find significant differences between the number of potentially controversial titles and the number of randomly selected titles found in the New Jersey public library collections.

Personal Characteristics of Librarians

In a discussion of the profession of librarianship, Goode (1961: 316–318) observed that "in a high but unknown percentage of instances, the librarian does not buy the books which might arouse local critics. There is a wide discrepancy between values and practices." Speculating about the reasons for the librarian's timidity in selection, Downs (1984: 8) suggested that "perhaps psychologists and psychiatrists may be able to offer explanations for the state of mind which produces censorship pressures." Broderick (1983: 44), also speculating, wondered whether censors have achieved the formal-operations stage in cognitive development. Fiske (1959: 15) concluded that "inspired idealism" and a "concept of moral commitment" provided the best defenses against censorship pressures.

One of the factors contributing to the protection of freedom to read identified by Fiske (1959: 25) was the perceived autonomy of librarians.

> Among those school librarians who believe that responsibility [for final selection decisions] should be vested in the librarian, half feel that in the event of a flare-up over controversial materials their own authority should be superseded by that of faculty, administration, or supervisory personnel in the office of the superintendent.

Ambivalence about selection decisions was further illustrated by Fiske's finding that school librarians who favored centralization of selection looked upon centralized selection as a protective device. These librarians tended to be cautious in their own book selection practices and least outspoken on freedom-to-read issues. Those who strongly opposed centralized selection were also likely to resist restrictive pressures (Fiske 1959: 26–31). "Autonomy in book selection does not, in fact, exist in metropolitan high schools; but with lack of autonomy comes increase in protection."

Discussing the legal rights of students, parents, teachers, administrators, and librarians, O'Neil (1981: 138–161) pointed out the scarcity of court cases defining the rights of librarians and libraries. Unlike publishers or movie producers with an economic stake in pursuing retribution in the courts, librarians have not pursued legal action as a remedy for censorship. Furthermore, though librarians were not highly paid, they were usually not indigent, and thus did not have recourse to legal aid. But O'Neil suggested that while such factors might have played a role in the lack of legal precedent, perhaps "the traditionally passive nature of the library profession may in part have kept its members from seeking legal support." O'Neil suggested that while librarians have "historically been reluctant to press for a redress of grievances," they are also "uneasy about being exposed to public scrutiny," which might endanger their reputations and jeopardize their employment. O'Neil reported a "substantial amount of self-censorship by librarians fearful of reprimands or reprisals."

Hentoff (1980: 294) also observed the reluctance of librarians to risk public scrutiny. Hentoff noted that "in certain cities or towns . . . librarians, fearful of somehow offending 'community standards' and thereby being punished, may censor themselves and stock only those books . . . which are not likely to offend anyone." Woods and Salvatore (1981) asked whether there was a strong enough mechanism in the profession to make sure that job security was protected during censorship situations.

Demographic Variables

Fiske (1959: 68, 128) found that factors such as training and professional affiliation were more pertinent than pressures from patrons, local groups, or other influences in identifying restrictive librarians. However, among school librarians, professional training was not found to be so decisive as among public librarians. Librarians with more extensive educational backgrounds were found by Pope to be less restrictive than librarians with less training (1974: 165).

Both Pope (1974: 180) and Fiske (1959: 129) reported that librarians with fewer years experience were less restrictive than librarians with more experience. Seventy-six percent of the librarians who had worked twenty or more years "habitually avoided" or "sometimes avoided" controversial material, compared with 44 percent of the librarians who had less than ten years experience. Farley (1964: 137) also discovered that experienced librarians in Nassau County had a tendency to be more restrictive than inexperienced librarians.

Membership in professional organizations does not guarantee adherence to freedom-to-read principles. Fiske (1959) reported that librarians active in local, state, and national professional organizations fell into a middle category between habitual avoidance and never taking controversy into account in their selection decisions. In contrast, individuals who did not belong to professional associations tended not to take controversy into account. "By design or by accident, exposure to professional organizations seems to be conducive to the kinds of compromises in book selection that can be professionally rationalized" (Fiske 1959: 68).

Woods and Salvatore (1981: 106–108) used a sample of librarians from the American Association of School Librarians for their study of self-censorship in collection development and expected to find less evidence of self-censorship because of the professional concern demonstrated by membership in a national professional association. They concluded, however, that their subjects seemed to be avoiding controversial titles. The large numbers of materials on restricted access showed a

"reluctance of many librarians to face censorship battles."
Serebnick (1982) questioned the conclusions of these researchers and pointed out that not purchasing a title on a
checklist did not necessarily point to self-censorship by the
librarian. Other factors might have accounted for the missing
titles, or the research design might have been flawed.

Gender was not found to be a factor in the Bundy and
Stakem (1982) survey of public librarians, but Busha (1971:
98) found a statistically significant difference between male
and female public librarians in their attitudes toward censorship and intellectual freedom. Male librarians agreed more
with intellectual freedom principles, and male librarians were
found to be more opposed to censorship. England (1974)
reported that females were more censorious than males in
book selection, but not in overall censorship activities, such as
circulation and labeling. Pope (1974: 180) found that female
librarians in school, public, and academic libraries were more
restrictive than male librarians in the three types of libraries.
Although more female librarians are employed in smaller
communities than larger communities, Busha did not report
gender differences related to size of community.

Contradictory conclusions have been reached about the
size of community and censorship. Busha found that 73
percent of the pro-censorship librarians were employed in
communities with populations of less than 35,000. However,
Fiske concluded that the degree of bureaucracy, not the size
of the community, was a decisive factor in censorship decisions. School librarians in metropolitan systems were not so
likely to order controversial materials as school librarians in
smaller communities.

SUMMARY

Studies investigating censorship and the attitudes of librarians toward intellectual freedom and censorship suggest that
while librarians articulate adherence to the intellectual freedom principles advocated by their profession, in practice they
do not always follow the principles of their profession.
Research on both school and public librarians provides

evidence of self-censorship. Pro-censorship attitudes and activities have been connected to age, sex, professional affiliation, type of materials, and selection of materials in school and public librarians, and authoritarian personalities in public librarians.

REFERENCES

Ahrens, Nyla Herber. "Censorship and the Teacher of English: A Questionnaire Survey of a Selected Sample of Secondary School Teachers of English." Doctoral dissertation, Columbia University, 1965.

American Association of School Librarians. *Information Power: Guidelines for School Library Media Programs.* Chicago: American Association of School Librarians and Association for Educational Communications and Technology, 1988.

American Association of School Librarians. *Media Programs: District and School.* Chicago: American Library Association and Association for Educational Communications and Technology, 1975.

American Association of School Librarians. *Standards for School Library Programs.* Chicago: American Library Association, 1960.

American Association of School Librarians. *Standards for School Media Programs.* Chicago and Washington, D.C.: American Library Association and National Education Association, 1969.

American Library Association. *Handbook of Organization.* Chicago: American Library Association, 1988.

American Library Association. *Intellectual Freedom Manual.* 3d ed. Chicago: American Library Association, 1989.

Association of American Publishers. *Limiting What Students Shall Read: Books and Other Learning Materials in Our Public Schools: How They Are Selected and How They Are Removed.* Washington, D.C.: American Association of Publishers, American Library Association, Association for Supervision and Curriculum Development, 1981.

Broderick, Dorothy. "Adolescent Development and Censorship." In *School Library Media Annual 1983,* Vol. 1. Aaron, Shirley, and Pat Scales, eds. Littleton, Colorado: Libraries Unlimited, 1983, 43–53.

Bump, Myrna Marlene. "Censorship Practiced by High School

Librarians Prior to (Actual) Book Selection." Doctoral dissertation, Kansas State University, 1980.

Bundy, Mary Lee, and Teresa Stakem. "Librarians and Intellectual
Freedom: Are Opinions Changing?" *Wilson Library Bulletin* 57
(April, 1982), 584–589.

Burress, Lee. "Censorship in School Libraries." *ALA Yearbook 1983*
Chicago: American Library Association, 1983, 246–247.

Burress, Lee. "Summary Report of a Survey of Censorship Pressures on the American High School, 1982." Urbana, Illinois:
National Council of Teachers of English, 1983.

Burress, Lee. "Censorship in Wisconsin Public High Schools." *How
Censorship Affects the School and Other Essays*. Racine: Wisconsin Council of Teachers of English, 1984, 60–101.

Busha, Charles H. "The Attitudes of Midwestern Public Librarians
Toward Intellectual Freedom and Censorship." Doctoral dissertation, Indiana University, 1971.

Busha, Charles H. *Freedom Versus Suppression and Censorship: With
a Study of the Attitudes of Midwestern Public Librarians and a
Bibliography of Censorship*. Littleton, Colorado: Libraries Unlimited, 1972.

Douma, Rollin. "Censorship in the English Classroom: A Review of
Research." *Journal of Research and Development in Education* 9
(1976), 60–68.

Downs, Robert B. "Freedom of Speech and Press: Development of
a Concept." *Library Trends* 19 (1970), 8–18.

Downs, Robert B., and Ralph E. McCoy, eds. *The First Freedom
Today: Critical Issues Relating to Censorship and Intellectual
Freedom*. Chicago: American Library Association, 1984.

England, Claire St. Clere. "The Climate of Censorship in Ontario."
Doctoral dissertation, University of Toronto, 1974.

Farley, John J. "Book Censorship in the Senior High Libraries of
Nassau County, New York." Doctoral dissertation, New York
University, 1964.

Fiske, Marjorie (Lowenthal). *Book Selection and Censorship: A Study
of School and Public Librarians in California*. Berkeley: University of California Press, 1959.

Flagg, Wilma T. "Internal Censorship of Periodicals by Missouri
School Librarians in Grades 9–12." Master's thesis, Central
Missouri State University, 1986.

Goode, William J. "Librarianship from Occupation to Profession."
Library Quarterly 31 (October, 1961), 316–318.

Hentoff, Nat. *First Freedom: The Tumultuous History of Free Speech
in America*. New York: Delacorte, 1980.

Hopkins, Diane. "Censorship of School Library Materials and Its Implications." In *School Library Media Annual 1984,* Vol 2. Aaron, Shirley, and Pat Scales, eds. Littleton, Colorado: Libraries Unlimited, 1984, 9–22.

Jenkinson, Edward. *Censors in the Classroom: The Mind Benders.* Carbondale: Southern Illinois University Press, 1979.

McDonald, Fran. *A Report of a Survey on Censorship in Public Elementary and High School Libraries and Public Libraries in Minnesota.* Minneapolis: Minnesota Civil Liberties Union, 1983.

National Coalition Against Censorship. "Books on Trial: A Survey of Recent Cases." New York: National Coalition Against Censorship, 1985.

National Commission on Libraries and Information Science. "Censorship Activities in Public and Public School Libraries, 1975–1985." A Report to the Senate Subcommittee on Appropriations for the Departments of Labor, Health and Human Services, and Education and Related Agencies. U.S. National Commission on Libraries and Information Science. March, 1986.

O'Neil, Robert M. *Classrooms in the Crossfire: The Rights of Students, Parents, Teachers, Administrators, Librarians and the Community.* Bloomington: Indiana University Press, 1981.

Pope, Michael. *Sex and the Undecided Librarian: A Study of Librarians' Opinions on Sexually Oriented Literature.* Metuchen, New Jersey: Scarecrow Press, 1974.

Serebnick, Judith. "An Analysis of the Relationship Between Book Reviews and the Inclusion of Potentially Controversial Books in Public Libraries." *Collection Building* 1 (1979), 8–53.

Serebnick, Judith. "Book Reviews and the Selection of Potentially Controversial Books in Public Libraries." *Library Quarterly* 51 (October, 1981), 390–409.

Serebnick, Judith. "Self-Censorship by Librarians: An Analysis of Checklist-Based Research." *Drexel Library Quarterly* 18 (Winter, 1982), 35–56.

Watson, Jerry J., and Bill C. Snider. "Book Selection Pressures on School Library Media Specialists and Teachers." *School Media Quarterly* 9 (Winter, 1981), 95–101.

Woods, L. B. *A Decade of Censorship in America: The Threat to Classroom and Libraries.* Metuchen, New Jersey: Scarecrow Press, 1979.

Woods, L. B., and Lucy Salvatore. "Self-Censorship in Collection

Development by High School Library Media Specialists."
School Media Quarterly 9 (Winter, 1981), 102–108.
Woodworth, Mary. *Intellectual Freedom, the Young Adult, and Schools: A Wisconsin Study.* Madison: University of Wisconsin, 1976.

CHAPTER 3
MORAL DEVELOPMENT: RELATED LITERATURE

Psychologists using developmental theories of human growth and maturity suggest that there are stages through which individuals progress in areas of cognitive development, moral reasoning, and ego strength. This study investigated the relationship between one of these developmental theories—moral reasoning—and attitudes toward intellectual freedom and censorship held by secondary school librarians. Specifically, the research examined the relationship between moral development described by Lawrence Kohlberg and attitudes toward intellectual freedom and censorship. According to Kohlberg (1971: 202), stages five and six, the principled level of moral reasoning, are based in constitutional democracy, including a bill of rights protecting individual liberties. The core of justice is liberty or civil rights, united by respect for the freedoms of others.

MORALITY

According to Rest (1986: 3), morality refers to "a particular type of social value, that having to do with how humans cooperate and coordinate their activities in the service of furthering human welfare, and how they adjudicate conflicts among individual interests." Shweder, Turiel, and Much (1981: 290) described the formal criteria that define morality.

> Prescriptions will be classified as moral if they are (1) *obligatory*, that is, duties are invoked that do not depend on what anyone happens to want to do, (2) *generalizable*

or just, that is, what is right or wrong for one is right or
wrong for any similar person in similar circumstances,
and (3) *important,* that is, the moral has precedence. If
we subdivide "obligation" into some of its components,
moral prescriptions are also perceived as (4) *impersonal
or external,* that is, what is right or wrong is right or
wrong regardless of whether people recognize it as such,
(5) *unalterable,* that is, what is right or wrong cannot be
changed by consensus or legislation, and (6) *ahistorical,*
that is, although its recognition may be historical, there
is no point in time at which the validity of what is right
or wrong changes.

Decisions about access to information made by librarians
adhering to their professional ethic follow the criteria described by Shweder et al.: that is, providing unrestricted
access is obligatory, generalizable, important, and impersonal.

Moral Behavior

Rest (1982: 559) outlined a four-component framework
from which to view the process leading to moral behavior.

The production of moral behavior in a particular
situation involves (1) interpreting the situation in terms
of how people's welfare is affected by possible actions of
the subject. (2) figuring out what the ideally moral
course of action would be. (3) selecting among valued
outcomes to intend to do the moral course of action. and
(4) executing and implementing what one intends to do.

The four components were described as interpreting,
defining, deciding, and acting. In the first component, an
individual interprets the situation and uses a combination of
affect and cognition to analyze how the situation will affect
self and others. In the second component, the individual
defines what ought to be done, what is morally right, and
focuses on the reasoning or rationale for a course of action. In
component 3 the individual balances competing values and
decides the morally right action. Carrying out the selected

plan of action constitutes component 4. Perseverance, resoluteness, competence, character, and ego strength influence the action. According to Rest, the cognitive processes used in determining the moral course of action—component 2— involve moral reasoning. These components illustrate the process followed by librarians in making decisions about access.

Kohlberg Theory of Moral Development

The Kohlberg theory of moral development posits that there is a universal, invariant sequence through which individuals move in developing moral maturity. Based on Piaget's cognitive and moral development research, Kohlberg's research began in 1958 with his dissertation and continued with a longitudinal study of a group of seventy-two boys aged 10 to 16. Moral reasoning was characterized as dealing with questions of fairness, justice, and social cooperation. Kohlberg described a moral situation as "one involving issues of justice, that is, a conflict of rights or claims" (Kohlberg and Candee 1984: 541). Kohlberg further described justice as a basic and universal standard, and defined the core of justice as "the distribution of rights and duties regulated by concepts of equality and reciprocity" (Kohlberg 1984: 184).

Moral development progresses over three levels: preconventional, in which moral development is characterized by the individual needs of the people involved; conventional, in which moral development is characterized by group or social relationships; and postconventional or principled, in which moral development is characterized by application of universal concepts of fairness and justice. At the conventional level, conflicts are resolved in group or social terms, rather than in individual terms, whereas at the preconventional level, moral dilemmas are viewed in terms of the individual. At the postconventional level, moral dilemmas are viewed in terms of universal justice and fairness, regardless of the individual or group involved. Within each level, Kohlberg described stages that indicate the orientation of the individual.

I. **Preconventional Level**

  Stage 1: The punishment and obedience orientation
  Stage 2: The instrumental–relativist orientation

II. **Conventional Level**

  Stage 3: The interpersonal concordance or "good boy–nice girl" orientation
  Stage 4: The "law and order" orientation

III. **Postconventional, Autonomous, or Principled Level**

  Stage 5: The social–contract, legalistic orientation
  Stage 6: The universal ethical principle orientation

(A detailed outline of Kohlberg's stages of moral development is provided in Appendix B.)

RESEARCH IN MORAL DEVELOPMENT

Three phases of moral development research have been identified. Kohlberg (1979) described the first phase beginning with his dissertation in 1958 as research that "delineated the broad outlines of culturally universal qualitative patterns of moral judgment." The second phase, primarily methodological, resulted in two methods of measuring moral judgment: the Harvard scoring method—a reliable, but lengthy and complex interview scoring method; and the Minnesota *DIT*—a reliable and valid objective test. Rest (1979) identified the third phase of moral development research as exploring the experiences and characteristics of individuals related to moral reasoning.

Additional research explored moral judgment relationships to attitudes. Rest (1975: 83–84) provided two reasons for such research: first, to seek evidence that "moral judgment is not just a value-neutral intellectualizing skill or style, but that it relates to value commitments as well as to purely cognitive capacities" and second, an interest in relating responses in hypothetical situations to current value controversies.

Rest (1979: 3) commented on the number of studies on moral development.

> Major social events have focused attention on moral issues. The Civil Rights movement, the student protests, the Vietnam War, Watergate, the women's movement all have emphasized issues of social justice, thus making it difficult for thoughtful people not to be concerned about morality.

These social events, combined with attention to the study of cognition by psychologists, created an opportune time for research on the theory of moral development and, no doubt, contributed to the hundreds of studies focusing on the concept of moral development.

More than five hundred studies have been conducted using the *Defining Issues Test*. No attempt was made to review all of them. Rather, selected studies related to the hypotheses specific to this investigation were reviewed. Librarians adhere to the tenet that the personal, social, religious, and political beliefs and values of the individual librarian are not valid criteria to use when selecting resources. Instead, universal rights of access to information based on the First Amendment govern the access decisions of librarians. This literature review focused on moral development studies using the *Defining Issues Test (DIT)* related to personal values and beliefs in which religion, political activism, ideology, and life experiences were identified as variables.

Moral Development and Speech

The principles of unrestricted access to information advocated by the library profession are rooted in the freedom of speech clause of the First Amendment. The connection between moral reasoning and free speech has been described in discussions of the implications of moral development decision making and in reports of research.

Rest (1975: 89) stated that "from society's perspective, principled moral judgment is presupposed in the functioning of a democracy" and pointed out that "the difference between conventional moral thinking and principled moral thinking is crucial in people's judgment of many current public policy issues." Candee (1980: 175), writing about liberty, asserted that "the ability to make one's own decisions and to pursue one's inclinations necessarily includes the freedoms of speech, assembly, and action."

Rest (1982: 557) pointed out that moral problems "involve finding some balance between competing claims and interests." Adhering to the tenets of the "Library Bill of Rights" involves balancing competing interests for librarians. For example, librarians must resolve conflicts between their personal views and their selection decisions. Librarians must resolve conflicts between the patron's right of access to information and outside pressures to restrict certain information.

Based on an earlier study that "demonstrated that moral reasoning is indeed related to political activism, at least of the left-wing variety," O'Connor (1980: 237–255) found that postconventional moral reasoners were "more likely to disapprove of limiting freedom of speech for anyone" than conventional moral reasoners among students in three European universities (English, Scottish, and French). Conventional moral reasoning correlated negatively with support of freedom of speech ranging in significance from $-.17$ (significant at the .05 level) to $-.44$ (significant at the .0001 level). O'Connor (1980: 254) concluded that "moral reasoning . . . is a measurable variable that can help political scientists understand political attitudes and behavior and may even be essential to that understanding."

Moral Development and Liberalism

The connection between Kohlberg's theory and liberalism was discussed by several commentators on moral development. Reid and Yanarella (1980: 107–132) suggested that "support for Kohlberg's schema springs from the dominant values (and their forms) of Western liberalism (American style)." Spence (1980: 161) described Kohlberg as a man of some "liberality" who "values democracy, freedom, equality, fairness, and individualism." The connection between political liberalism and moral development was also made by Sullivan (1977) in a critical analysis of the liberal ideological underpinnings of the Kohlberg theory. Sullivan suggested that the theory had been developed in an era receptive to its constructs and that the theory had served to fill a vacuum in the area of values. The "decade of the sixties demanded theories that dealt with both intellectual and moral progress. . . . In a culture deeply involved in moral problems related to race, poverty, and war this theory offered a concept of justice which promised to deal with the quagmire of value relativity." Thus, according to Sullivan, the theory addressed needs of conscience, termed "liberal" freedom of conscience.

However, using a political self-rating, Getz (1985) did not find support for the thesis that the moral development theory is strongly correlated with liberal thought. She found that support for human rights was more strongly related to moral reasoning than to an index of political ideology.

Rest (1986) responded to the criticism that the theory of moral development reflected the liberal end of a liberal/ conservative continuum by reporting the results of an experiment in which subjects were instructed to fake like a liberal (radical) on the *Defining Issues Test.* In attempting to follow these instructions, subjects increased the number of A (angry, antiestablishment-sounding) items they selected. When the limited number of A items was exhausted, subjects were forced to select P (principled moral reasoning) items. To verify this conclusion, Barnett (1985) expanded the experiment by increasing the number of available A items and found that, when more A items were available, subjects continued to select them rather than P items.

Human Rights

Getz (1985) investigated the relationship between support of human rights and principled moral reasoning. Examining subjects from church congregations and volunteer students, Getz found a significant relationship between principled moral reasoning and support of human rights. Subjects using principled reasoning were more consistent in their support of human rights for all persons generally than were subjects using conventional reasoning.

Religion

Rest (1979) cited a study by Ernsberger, who had analyzed written documents from different religions and found that written materials and official statements from liberal religions illustrated more principled thinking than similar documents from more conservative religions. Members and lay leaders of liberal and conservative congregations showed significantly different moral reasoning scores (P scores). Conservative church members and lay leaders had lower P scores than members and lay leaders from more liberal congregations. Getz (1985) found a negative correlation of −.47 between conservative religious ideology and the P score and a positive correlation of .53 with stage 4 (law and order) reasoning. She found that liberal religious ideology was a strong predictor of principled moral reasoning.

Similarly, Lawrence (1978) found that seminarians holding conservative religious views differed from philosophers and ninth graders. Lawrence asked subjects to "think aloud" while deciding the importance of a set of moral dilemma items. She found that subjects could process items on the DIT without using moral criteria at all. Philosophers used more propositions to identify issues and weigh alternatives, ninth graders focused more on story information and practicalities, while seminarians used more religious criteria in processing the items. Principled and nonprincipled criteria, practical considerations, issues, and stimuli accounted for 52 percent of propositions. Moral criteria accounted for 25 percent of the propositions voiced by the subjects.

Shaver (1984) conducted a longitudinal study of students at a religious Bible college and concluded that the environment at the Bible college fostered stage 4 reasoning and offered little stimulation for development of the more relativistic stage 5 reasoning. Bible college students showed greatest preference for stage 4 reasoning, while liberal arts students appeared to make the transition from stage 4 to stage 5 during college years.

Hay (1982) found significantly higher P scores among a group of volunteer conscientious objectors based on a personal moral code than among subjects basing objection on religion at the college and graduate level (p <.005), but not at the high school level. Conscientious objectors were found to have significantly higher P scores (p <.0005) at each educational level, when compared with the means of Rest's subjects at similar educational levels.

Moral Development and Life Experiences

Barnett and Volker (1985) analyzed ten life experience studies and found evidence to connect higher levels of moral reasoning with knowledge of, and activity in, certain life experiences. In five of eight studies, experience with social issues and political activities were found to be positively related to moral judgment. Following and expanding the Barnett and Volker research, Deemer (1985) designed an exploratory study to isolate life experience variables that might contribute to moral judgment development in adult populations. Using interview techniques, Deemer explored life experience variables and concluded that academic variables emerged as most important. Deemer found that higher moral reasoning scores were associated with individuals living and or working in an intellectually stimulating environment. Deemer concluded that individuals who showed civic responsibility and political awareness and experienced continued intellectual stimulation showed increases in adult moral judgment. These persons were described as "individuals who like to read, who grapple with issues and ideas, who show a desire to learn, and surround themselves with others who are intellectually oriented." In other words, a combination of environmental and personal factors were found to contribute to increases in moral judgment in adults.

Moral Development and Demographic Characteristics

Kohlberg (1980: 60) asserted that from 10 to 20 percent of the adult population achieved stages 5 and 6 of moral development and only 5 percent arrived at stage 6. Age and education appear to be the the most significant variables in adult population differences in moral reasoning.

Age/Education. Rest (1986: 106) stated that "in American samples it is now well documented that DIT scores increase with age/education shifts." Rest (1979) combined adult subjects from 29 samples and found an average P score of 40 and observed that adults "do not show much advance beyond that accounted for by their level of education." Another examination of combined student groups showed that P scores "increase about ten points with each increase in level of education." From a secondary analysis of 4,500 subjects, Rest concluded that formal education accounted for 38 percent to 49 percent of variance of *DIT* scores.

Based on a review of longitudinal, cross-sectional studies, Rest, Davison, and Robbins (1978: 268) observed that there is no

> clear expectation based on theory on how various adult age groups will score on the DIT. . . . Development in moral judgment seems to advance dramatically as long as a person is in school, and that when a person discontinues formal education, his moral judgment development tends to stabilize. . . . Adults in general seem to slow down in moral judgment development in their 20s and to plateau after leaving school; however, those continuing their education in specialities that emphasize moral thinking (doctoral students in moral philosophy or political science, seminarians) attain much higher DIT scores than the average adult.

Gender Differences. Kohlberg's theory has been criticized as being gender specific. Discussions of gender bias in the theory of moral development focused on three issues: (1) the original research was conducted with a male sample, and thus the theory was developed by a male using male subjects;

(2) the moral dilemmas feature male actors; and (3) adult females appeared to attain lower scores than males in some studies. The most widely publicized criticism was voiced by Gilligan (1978), who proposed that male and female social development results in two moral orientations, one of justice (male) and one of care (female). Gilligan suggested that differences in moral orientation might account for differences in scores between male and female subjects. Subsequent research illustrated that males did not score higher on moral development measures. Rest (1986: 116) concluded that "there exists little evidence in DIT responses to suggest that males are better able to reason about hypothetical dilemmas, or that justice reasoning is in some way a male domain."

While gender differences received much theoretical attention, subsequent reviews of results of previous research and meta-analysis indicated that "there is now little to suggest that mean scores of male and female groups differ on justice oriented measures of moral development" (Thoma 1985: 18). "Formal education is 250 times more powerful than sex as a correlate" (Rest and Thoma 1985: 709–714). In a secondary analysis of 3,000 subjects, formal education accounted for 53 percent of variance in P scores, while sex accounted for only 0.2 percent.

SUMMARY

According to the Kohlberg theory of moral development, individuals develop moral maturity by progressing through three levels in an invariant, universal sequence. The three levels represent increasingly more principled ways of reasoning about moral issues. Reasoning at level one is based on the needs of the individual, level two reasoning is based in group norms, and level three is based on universal principles of justice. Access to information as defined in the "Library Bill of Rights" assumes the application of principles of justice for all users of the library. Moral reasoning has been found to be related to issues of speech and is essential for the operation of a democracy. Moral reasoning measured by the *Defining Issues Test* has been found to be related to age and education, but not to gender.

REFERENCES

Barnett, Robert, and Joseph M. Volker. "Moral Judgment and Life Experiences." Unpublished manuscript. Minneapolis: University of Minnesota, 1985.

Blasi, Augusto. "Bridging Moral Cognition and Moral Action: A Critical Review of the Literature." *Psychological Bulletin* 88 (July, 1980): 1–45.

Candee, Daniel. "The Moral Psychology of Watergate and Its Aftermath." In Wilson, Richard W., and Gordon J. Schochet. *Moral Development and Politics.* New York: Praeger, 1980, 172–189.

Colby, Anne, and Lawrence Kohlberg. "Invariant Sequence and Internal Consistency in Moral Judgment Stages." In Kurtines, William M., and Jacob Gewirtz. *Morality, Moral Behavior, and Moral Development.* New York: John Wiley, 1984, 41–51.

Deemer, Deborah K. "Research in Moral Education." Chicago: American Educational Research Association, 1985.

Getz, Irene Rose. "Moral Reasoning, Religion, and Attitudes Toward Human Rights." Doctoral dissertation, University of Minnesota, 1985.

Getz, Irene Rose. "The Relation of Moral and Religious Ideology to Human Rights." Unpublished manuscript. Minneapolis: University of Minnesota, n.d.

Gilligan, Carol. "In a Different Voice: Women's Conceptions of Self and of Morality." *Harvard Educational Review* 47 (1977), 481–517.

Hay, James. "A Study of Principled Moral Reasoning Within a Sample of Conscientious Objectors." *Moral Education Forum* 7 (1982), 1–8.

Kohlberg, Lawrence. "Foreword." Rest, James R. *Development in Judging Moral Issues.* Minneapolis: University of Minnesota Press, 1979, vii–xvi.

Kohlberg, Lawrence. "From Is to Ought: How to Commit the Naturalistic Fallacy and Get Away with It in the Study of Moral Development." In Mischel, T., ed. *Cognitive Develop-*

ment and Epistemology. New York: Academic Press, 1971, 151–236.

Kohlberg, Lawrence. *The Psychology of Moral Development,* Vol. 2: *Essays on Moral Development.* San Francisco: Harper and Row, 1984.

Kohlberg, Lawrence, and Daniel Candee. "The Relationship of Moral Judgment to Moral Action." In Kohlberg, Lawrence. *The Psychology of Moral Development.* San Francisco: Harper and Row, 1984, 498–581.

Kohlberg, Lawrence, and Clark Power. "Moral Development, Religious Thinking, and the Question of a Seventh Stage." *Zygon* 16 (1981), 203–259.

Kohlberg, Lawrence, and Richard H. Hersh. "Moral Development: A Review of the Theory." *Theory into Practice* 16 (1977), 53–59.

McGeorge, Colin. "Some Correlates of Principled Moral Thinking in Young Adults." *Journal of Moral Education* 5 (1976), 265–273.

O'Connor, Robert E. "Parental Sources and Political Consequences of Levels of Moral Reasoning Among European University Students." In Wilson, Richard W., and Gordon J. Schochet. *Moral Development and Politics.* New York: Praeger, 1980, 237–255.

Reid, Herbert G., and Ernest J. Yanarella. "The Tyranny of the Categorical: On Kohlberg and the Politics of Moral Development." In Wilson, Richard W., and Gordon Schochet. *Moral Development and Politics.* New York: Praeger, 1980, 107–132.

Rest, James R. *Development in Judging Moral Issues.* Minneapolis: University of Minnesota Press, 1979.

Rest, James R. *Moral Development: Advances in Research and Theory.* New York: Praeger, 1986.

Rest, James R. "Morality." In Flavell, J., and E. Markman, eds. *Cognitive Development,* Vol. 4: *Manual of Child Psychology.* Mussen, P., ed. New York: Wiley, 1982, 556–629.

Rest, James R. "A Psychologist Looks at the Teaching of Ethics." *Hastings Center Report* (February, 1982), 29–36.

Rest, James R. "Recent Research on an Objective Test of Moral Judgement: How the Important Issues of a Moral Dilemma Are Defined." In DePalma, David J., and Jeanne M. Foley. *Moral Development: Current Theory and Research.* Hillsdale, New Jersey: Lawrence Erlbaum, 1975, 75–93.

Rest, James R. *Revised Manual for the Defining Issues Test.* Minneapolis: Minnesota Moral Research Projects, 1979.

Rest, James R., Mark L. Davison, and Steven Robbins. "Age Trends in Judging Moral Issues: A Review of Cross-sectional, Longitudinal, and Sequential Studies of the Defining Issues Test." *Child Development* 49 (1978), 263–279.

Rest, James, Deborah Deemer, et al. "Life Experiences and Developmental Pathways." In Rest, James R. *Moral Development: Advances in Reseach and Theory*. New York: Praeger, 1986, 28–58.

Rest, James R., and Stephen J. Thoma. "Relation of Moral Judgment Development to Formal Education." *Developmental Psychology* 21 (1985), 709–714.

Shaver, Darrel G. "A Longitudinal Investigation of the Moral Development of Selected Students at a Conservative Religious College." Doctoral dissertation, University of Iowa, 1984.

Shweder, Richard A., Eliot Turiel, and Nancy C. Much. "The Moral Intuitions of the Child." In Flavell, John H., and Lee Ross. *Social Cognitive Development: Frontiers and Possible Futures*. Cambridge: Cambridge University Press, 1981, 288–305.

Spence, Larry D. "Moral Judgment and Bureaucracy." In Wilson, Richard W., and Gordon J. Schochet. *Moral Development and Politics*. New York: Praeger, 1980, 137–171.

Sullivan, E. V. "A Study of Kohlberg's Structural Theory of Moral Development: A Critique of Liberal Social Science Ideology." *Human Development* 20 (1977), 352–376.

Thoma, Stephen J. "Estimating Gender Differences in the Comprehension and Preference of Moral Issues." Unpublished manuscript. Minneapolis: University of Minnesota, 1985.

CHAPTER 4
DESIGN OF THE ATTITUDE STUDY

Assuming that developmental characteristics might influence application of the concepts of the "Library Bill of Rights," a study was designed to examine attitudes toward intellectual freedom and censorship and one developmental characteristic: moral reasoning. The purpose of the study was to examine the relationships among attitudes of secondary school librarians in Iowa, Minnesota, and Wisconsin toward intellectual freedom and censorship and selected demographic variables and attitudes toward intellectual freedom and censorship and one developmental variable: principled moral reasoning.

RELATIONSHIPS AMONG THE MAJOR VARIABLES

The rationale for selecting moral reasoning as the developmental variable to examine can be described by discussing relationships among the major variables. Kohlberg's theory of moral development addresses issues of justice and rights. Rights are defined in terms of general individual rights and standards that have been constitutionally and democratically agreed upon. Candee (1980) pointed out that these rights necessarily include freedom of speech. Rest (1975) studied the association between moral reasoning and libertarian attitudes and identified an "arena of 'real-life' behavior" related to moral reasoning that included taking stands on value issues. Each moral judgment stage is found to have distinctive ways of defining value issues and making decisions about what do to. In a study of levels of moral reasoning among European university students, O'Connor (1980) found a positive correlation between freedom of speech and postconventional moral reasoning and a negative correlation between freedom of speech and conventional reasoning.

Kohlberg and Candee (1984: 516, 541) suggested that moral situations involve "a conflict between a standard or norm that the individual accepts as being right and some other value or norm." They defined a moral situation as "one involving issues of justice, that is, a conflict of rights or claims." Censorship situations and decisions about allowing or restricting access to resources and ideas constitute moral situations. In a typical challenge situation, the librarian's responsibility to provide resources representing a variety of points of view conflicts with the wishes of a parent or group to limit access to a particular point of view. When a parent wants the school to remove a resource, there is a conflict between the right of one parent to monitor the reading, viewing, or listening of his or her child and the right of other children to have access to the information and ideas contained in the challenged resource. Likewise, librarians who use their personal beliefs as a reason for selecting or rejecting resources are in conflict with the rights of patrons to locate those resources.

Perhaps school librarians, while agreeing theoretically with the principles of intellectual freedom advocated by their profession, in practice make selection and retention decisions based upon factors other than professional judgment. Perhaps levels of moral reasoning influence the decisions made by librarians when faced with conflicting opinions as to the appropriateness of providing specific resources in a school library. Likewise, librarians might be influenced by their levels of moral reasoning when confronted with requests to remove resources from a school library.

Librarians reasoning at principled moral levels are likely to agree with intellectual freedom principles, and librarians reasoning at conventional levels might agree with restrictive practices. For example, persons reasoning at conventional levels might be influenced by authority figures or the wishes of individual library users when making selection decisions. Principled reasoning would enable librarians to understand the necessity of providing a variety of materials to meet the needs of most library users. Reasoning at principled levels, librarians would conclude that the right of all persons to have access to resources takes precedence over the right of any person, including the librarian, to limit resources based upon personal beliefs and values.

The study reported here illustrates the relationship between the principled moral reasoning of secondary school librarians and their attitudes toward intellectual freedom and censorship. While behavior cannot be predicted from attitudes, moral reasoning represents one of the factors that might influence the behavior of librarians in censorship situations.

RESEARCH QUESTIONS

Questions were formulated to examine relationships among the major variables: attitudes toward intellectual freedom and censorship, principled moral reasoning, geographical location, size of school, grade levels in school, age, sex, level of education, and membership in professional organizations.

1. Is there a relationship between attitudes of secondary school librarians toward intellectual freedom and attitudes toward censorship?
2. Is there a relationship between attitudes of secondary school librarians toward intellectual freedom and censorship and levels of moral reasoning?
3. Are there relationships between attitudes of secondary school librarians toward intellectual freedom and censorship and variables such as size of school, grade levels in school, geographical location of school district, age, sex, and educational level?
4. Are there relationships between membership in state and national professional organizations and attitudes toward intellectual freedom and censorship of secondary school librarians?

SUBJECTS

Secondary school librarians from Iowa, Minnesota, and Wisconsin were selected for this study. These three Midwestern states are contiguously located, similar in demographic characteristics, have a combination of urban and rural school districts and large and small high schools, and students in these three states consistently exhibit high scores in national tests. Further, limiting the geographical area to three states provided a manageable population. Secondary schools were defined as any combination of grades seven through twelve.

Identification of Sample

Lists of secondary school librarians were obtained from state departments of public instruction in the selected states. The list from the Minnesota State Department of Education did not include the names of the school librarians. Rather, Minnesota provided labels with the heading "Media Generalist" along with the address of the school and the city. Iowa and Wisconsin state departments provided names of media specialists along with addresses and schools. Additionally, while Iowa and Wisconsin names clearly indicated that the school had a school library and school librarian, the Minnesota list included every secondary school in the state. Thus, the Minnesota list included schools that did not have school librarians. Sampling procedures were affected by this lack of names from Minnesota. In reality, sampling in Minnesota was of secondary schools, rather than secondary school librarians. However, response rate did not appear to be affected.

After eliminating elementary school librarians from the Iowa list, the names acquired from state departments of public instruction were numbered and a table of random numbers was used to select the sample. A simple random sample was selected because of the homogeneous population (Leedy 1985: 156). One hundred fifty secondary school librarians were selected from each of the three states.

METHODS AND PROCEDURES

Survey research techniques were chosen as the method of collecting data. Random sampling procedures were used to identify the subjects. Secondary school librarians were selected for this study because of the incidence of censorship in secondary schools. Further, secondary school library collections were known to contain resources and topics that librarians might consider controversial, or that have been the object of censorship attempts in school districts.

Two previous research studies were used as models for this study. Both were attitude studies that used statements representing principles along with items applying the principles. One was a study by Getz (1985), who investigated the relationship between attitudes toward human rights and level of moral reasoning. Getz developed an instrument measuring attitudes toward "platitudes" about human rights and compared them with attitudes toward applying human rights principles. The second study was designed by Busha (1971), who compared attitudes toward the principles of intellectual freedom with attitudes toward applying the principles in public libraries.

Selection of Statistical Procedures

An exploratory study to examine relationships was appropriate for two reasons: first, little is known about the attitudes held by secondary school librarians toward intellectual freedom and censorship, and second, some secondary school librarians uphold the principles of their profession while others exhibit practices in violation of those principles. Relationships between attitudes toward intellectual freedom and censorship were examined, as were relationships among intellectual freedom, censorship, and principled levels of moral reasoning.

The Pearson product moment correlation method was used to analyze the data. The correlation method allowed the examination of relationships and also provided a measure of the strength of the relationships identified. In statistical terms, a correlation provides a numerical indication of the degree of relationship between two variables—in this case, the degree of relationship between scores on the *Intellectual Freedom/Censorship Attitude Scale* and scores on the *Defining Issues Test*. If scores show a positive linear relationship, as one score goes up so does the other. If scores show a negative linear relationship, as one score goes up, the other goes down. A perfect positive relationship is represented by a score of 1.00. The closer the correlation to a plus or minus 1.00, the closer the relationship between the variables. For example, correlations over .85 indicate close relationships between the variables being studied.

Further analysis of the data included t-tests to determine consistency between intellectual freedom scores and censorship scores, and analysis of variance on the demographic variables. The t-test showed whether the mean scores (average scores) on the *Intellectual Freedom Attitude Scale* were significantly different from the mean (average) scores on the *Censorship Attitude Scale*. Analysis of variance was used to compare mean scores when subjects fell into three or more groups, for example years of experience or size of school.

INSTRUMENTS

Two instruments were needed for the study: one to gather data about intellectual freedom and censorship attitudes and the other to measure level of moral reasoning. A paper-and-pencil moral reasoning test—the *Defining Issues Test*—was identified and permission received to use it. The attitude survey to measure intellectual freedom and censorship was developed and pretested for the study. Details about the *Defining Issues Test* and the development of the attitude survey used in this study are included in Chapter 5, "Data Collection Instruments."

ASSUMPTIONS

This study began with the assumption that school librarians would know the principles of intellectual freedom by virtue of studying professional documents in their professional preparation programs and continuing education activities. Another assumption was that the professional ethic stated in intellectual freedom documents is not the only influence on selection and censorship decisions. Other influences might include attitudes toward restrictive practices, the size and grade levels of the school, the perceived attitudes of other school personnel toward intellectual freedom and censorship, and perceptions of community values about intellectual freedom and censorship.

LIMITATIONS

As with any study, several limitations are recognized. The population studied was secondary school librarians in three Midwestern states. Findings cannot be generalized beyond secondary school librarians in these three states to all secondary school librarians, nor to elementary school librarians or public librarians.

A second limitation was the use of an attitude scale. There is no certainty that subjects' responses reflected their true attitudes. Subjects might have disguised their true attitudes on a scale designed to measure readily recognized professional principles.

Another limitation was inherent in the research design. This was an exploratory relationship study, not an experimental study. The findings indicated that the variables studied are related, not that certain variables represent causal factors. Behavior cannot be predicted from attitudes. Experimental research is needed to establish a causal connection between attitudes and behavior.

Moral reasoning was a major aspect of this study and the theory of moral development was accepted as it is currently being presented in the literature. The theory is evolving, and researchers do not all agree with the Kohlberg approach to defining moral reasoning. No attempt was made to critique the theory, nor to examine or explain commentary on the theory. The purpose of this study was to examine moral reasoning measured by the *Defining Issues Test*, not to join in the debate about the merits of various approaches to moral development.

The study was limited to principled moral reasoning and selected demographic characteristics, among the many that influence reactions to censorship situations. Further research is needed to identify other personal and demographic characteristics that influence the decisions made by school librarians in upholding the principles of freedom to read.

DEFINITION OF TERMS

Attitude. "An attitude is a mental and neural state of readiness, organized through experience, exerting a directive or dynamic influence upon the individual's response to all objects and situations with which it is related" (Allport 1967: 15).

Censorship. The removal of material from open access by any governing authority. This definition refers to removing resources from general use by any means solely for the purpose of restricting access to the ideas or information in the item. Censorship does not refer to removal of school library resources for administrative purposes, conditions of space, or because the item is obsolete or worn.

Challenge. A formal written expression of concern filed with the librarian or another school official questioning the presence and/or appropriateness of a specific resource. A challenge is not considered censorship.

Freedom to Read. Official statement expressing intellectual freedom principles adopted by the American Association of Publishers and the American Library Association. (A copy is provided in Appendix A.)

Intellectual Freedom. The broad definition stated in documents of the American Library Association refers to "the right of any person to hold any belief whatever on any subject, and to express such beliefs or ideas in whatever way the person believes appropriate" and the "right of unrestricted access to all information and ideas regardless of the medium of communication used" (American Library Association 1989: ix).

Library Bill of Rights. Official intellectual freedom statement of the American Library Association, approved 1939, adopted 1948, amended 1961, 1967, and 1980. (A copy is provided in Appendix A.)

Moral. Refers to a point of view that "stresses attributes of impartiality, universalizability, and the effort and willingness to come to agreement or consensus with other human beings in general about what is right" (Kohlberg 1984: 229).

Morality. Refers to a "particular type of social value: that having to do with how humans cooperate and coordinate their activities in the service of furthering human welfare, and how they adjudicate conflicts among individual interests" (Rest 1986: 3).

P Score. Measured by the *Defining Issues Test,* the P score represents the relative importance a person attributes to principled moral considerations in making a moral decision.

Principled Level. The level of moral reasoning at which "there is a clear effort to define moral values and principles that have validity and application apart from the authority of the groups or persons holding these principles and apart from the individual's own identification with these groups" (Kohlberg and Hersh 1977).

Prior Censorship. Decision not to acquire a resource based on reasons other than educational suitability or appropriate selection criteria. This decision could reflect the librarian's attitudes and beliefs or those of another person of authority in the school. *See also* Self-Censorship and Voluntary Censorship.

Restricted Collection. Resources that are separated from the general collection, located in a designated area, for purposes of controlling access, and limited in circulation to specified situations, conditions, or individuals.

School Librarian. Licensed professional who works in a school library media center. For the purposes of this research, the generic term *school librarian* was used rather than one of the several terms used in various states, such as *media specialist, media generalist,* or *school library media specialist.*

Selection. The process of identifying resources for purchase based on criteria related to the purposes of the library, the age and maturity of the users, and the needs of the curriculum in the school the library serves.

Self-Censorship. Removal, restriction, or failure to acquire resources for reasons other than those "encompassed in normal selection and circulation procedures" (Serebnick 1979: 12).

Voluntary Censorship. Removal or restriction of resources, or failure to acquire resources by the school librarian without pressure from other individuals or without being ordered to do so by a person in a position of authority over the school librarian.

Data Collection

The first survey was mailed during the spring of 1987. The mailing consisted of the ten-page questionnaire, a cover letter, and an addressed and stamped return envelope. A response of 59.11 percent was received from the first mailing. A second mailing, including another letter encouraging response, another copy of the survey, and another stamped and addressed return envelope, was sent to nonrespondents three weeks later. This second mailing increased the response rate to 73.55 percent. Because the end of the school year had arrived, the third envelope included a label requesting that the mailing be forwarded to the subject's home address. The third cover letter, emphasizing the importance of a response, pointed out that time to complete the survey might now be available. Another copy of the questionnaire and a stamped return envelope were included. The final response was 366 or 81.33 percent. This rate of response is considered high for a self-administered mail survey.

Thirty-eight intellectual freedom/censorship surveys were unusable or incomplete, making the response rate on that portion of the survey 72.88 percent. On the *Defining Issues Test (DIT)* portion of the survey, twenty-three subjects were rejected for having more than eight errors or two stories with inconsistencies. Twelve subjects, representing 9.56 percent of the sample, were rejected for checking more than eight M items. Eighty-three subjects were rejected because of missing ranks or ratings. Thus, 118 subjects, representing 32.2 percent of the sample, were rejected. The response rate then became 55.33 percent. Because of the big difference in response rate between subjects who completed all portions of the test and subjects who completed only the intellectual freedom/censorship portion, all analysis of intellectual freedom and censorship attitudes was conducted using the 72.88 percent response rate. The 55.33 percent response rate was used only for the analysis of the relationship between moral reasoning and attitudes toward censorship and intellectual freedom. Separate analyses were conducted to determine differences between individuals who were rejected because of failing the consistency check on the *DIT* and subjects who completed all portions of the survey. Not included in this total were four questionnaires: two from Minnesota returned because the schools had no school librarian, one returned as undeliverable, and one returned because the school librarian was deceased. Included in the questionnaires considered incomplete was a questionnaire returned by a school librarian employed part-time in two school districts.

Ethical Considerations

Throughout the investigation, considerable attention was given to protecting the privacy of subjects. Beginning with the letter of transmittal, confidentiality was promised to respondents. A note on privacy was included to assure potential respondents that the investigator was conscious of their right to privacy. The study required the collection of opinions of respondents to measure attitudes, and no deception or manipulation was involved. Participation in the study was voluntary. After the questionnaires were returned and responses recorded, the only identifying number remaining to connect a subject's name with a response was the number in the code indicating geographical location of respondent.

Further confidentiality was assured by employing a third person for data entry. Individual scores were combined to create group scores and means, and all analysis was done by computer. Discussion and reporting of findings involved only collective scores and means.

REFERENCES

Allport, Gordon W. "Attitudes." Reprinted in Jahoda, Marie, and Neil Warren, eds. *Attitudes: Selected Readings.* New York: Penguin Books, 1967, 15–21.

American Library Association. *Intellectual Freedom Manual.* 3d ed. Chicago: American Library Association, 1989.

Candee, Daniel. "The Moral Psychology of Watergate and Its Aftermath." In Wilson, Richard W., and Gordon J. Schochet. *Moral Development and Politics.* New York: Praeger, 1980, 172–189.

Kohlberg, Lawrence. *The Psychology of Moral Development,* Vol. 2: *Essays on Moral Development.* San Francisco: Harper and Row, 1984.

Kohlberg, Lawrence, and Daniel Candee. "The Relationship of Moral Judgment to Moral Action." In Kohlberg, Lawrence. *The Psychology of Moral Development.* San Francisco: Harper and Row, 1984, 498–581.

Kohlberg, Lawrence, and Richard H. Hersh. "Moral Development: A Review of the Theory." *Theory into Practice* 16 (1977), 53–59.

Leedy, Paul D. *Practical Research: Planning and Design.* 3d ed. New York: Macmillan, 1985.

O'Connor, Robert E. "Parental Sources and Political Consequences of Levels of Moral Reasoning Among European University Students." In Wilson, Richard W., and Gordon J. Schochet. *Moral Development and Politics.* New York: Praeger, 1980, 237–255.

Rest, James R. "Recent Research on an Objective Test of Moral Judgement: How the Important Issues of a Moral Dilemma Are Defined." In DePalma, David J., and Jeanne M. Foley. *Moral Development: Current Theory and Research.* Hillsdale, New Jersey: Lawrence Erlbaum, 1975, 75–93.

Rest, James R. *Moral Development: Advances in Research and Theory.* New York: Praeger, 1986.

Serebnick, Judith. "An Analysis of the Relationship Between Book Reviews and the Inclusion of Potentially Controversial Books in Public Libraries." *Collection Building* 1 (1979), 8–53.

CHAPTER 5
DATA COLLECTION INSTRUMENTS*

This research required instruments designed to collect data related to the major variables through a self-administered mail survey. A paper-and-pencil test was available to measure moral reasoning, but an appropriate instrument to measure intellectual freedom and censorship attitudes held by secondary school librarians was needed. Three factors were identified: (1) items were needed to determine attitudes toward intellectual freedom and also toward censorship; (2) librarians were to be surveyed about a sensitive area in which their practices might not reflect professional principles; and (3) the surveys were to be administered by mail, necessitating instruments of reasonable length.

MEASUREMENT OF INTELLECTUAL FREEDOM AND CENSORSHIP

Two instruments measuring attitudes toward intellectual freedom and censorship similar to the one needed for this investigation were identified. The first instrument was developed by Busha (1971) to survey the intellectual freedom attitudes of public librarians in the Midwest. Busha's instrument could not be adopted for this investigation for two reasons. First, the application items focused on practices in

---

*This chapter provides details about the data collection instruments. The process of developing and pretesting the *Intellectual Freedom/Censorship Attitude Scale* is included for individuals interested in that phase of research. Information about reliability of the instruments and scoring are included. Persons not interested in such matters might skip this chapter.

public libraries. For example, one item referred to the use of meeting rooms, and other items included fiction titles likely to be of concern in the early 1970s, but not at the present time in secondary school libraries. Next, while the "Freedom to Read" statement was still current, the 1967 "Library Bill of Rights," on which some of the intellectual freedom statements were based, had been revised in 1980. However, the Busha instrument was used as a model for constructing items, and six application items were revised or adapted for use in this study. Two of the items related to political literature and are discussed in another section of this chapter. The other four items included one about selecting fiction, another about the adverse publicity caused by a censorship incident, one dealing with flagging potentially controversial titles to alert users, and the last about the influence of court action on selecting a title for a library. The items in the Busha instrument were:

> Librarians should avoid purchasing works of fiction dealing with social, psychological, and sexual problems and concentrate more on building collections of non-offensive literary masterpieces.

> A censorship controversy is not worth the adverse public relations which it could cause for the library.

> Books which may offend standards of taste should be starred as a guide to those library patrons who wish to avoid these types of works.

> If your library has ordered a controversial book the reviews of which indicate that it is of literary merit but for which court action is now pending against another library in your state, you should cancel the order.

As revised and used in this instrument, the items were stated:

> Secondary school librarians should avoid purchasing works of fiction dealing with social, psychological, and sexual problems and concentrate more on building collections of classics.

A censorship controversy over a single book or magazine is not worth the adverse publicity that it could cause
for the school.

Books about controversial subjects should be starred as
a guide for students who wish to avoid works of this
type.

If a secondary school librarian has ordered a controversial but positively reviewed book, and now the book is
the object of court action in another school in the state,
the librarian should cancel the order.

The second instrument was developed by Woodworth for
a 1976 study in Wisconsin. Because the Woodworth instrument applied to classrooms and textbooks as well as to
libraries, most items were not applicable in the present
instance. Because an acceptable instrument had not been
identified, a new instrument was designed.

Major Considerations in Designing the Instrument

The intellectual freedom and censorship instrument had to
measure degree of agreement with professional principles
expressed in professional library association documents, and
also to measure degree of agreement with restrictive practices
in violation of professional principles. A major problem with
such an instrument was that librarians were likely to know the
"right" answers and could identify acceptable practice or ideal
behavior. Stemming from this problem was the potential
reluctance of professionals to agree with practices known to
be in violation of professional beliefs. However, it was
believed that an instrument could be designed in such a way
that agreement with intellectual freedom principles would
not necessarily preclude agreement with restrictive practices.
Strategies devised by Busha (1971: 31–35) in constructing an
instrument to measure similar attitudes among public librarians were followed. That is, some items allowed respondents
to project restrictive practices to others, and the Likert scale
provided for varying degrees of agreement or disagreement.

The objective was to design an instrument to measure agreement with intellectual freedom statements representing positions held by the profession of librarianship and attitudes held by school librarians toward restrictive practices or censorship. To measure intellectual freedom principles, phrases and sentences were taken from professional intellectual freedom documents. Statements were modified when necessary to reflect school libraries specifically, rather than libraries generally. For example, the statement, "Materials should not be excluded because of the origin, background, or views of those contributing to their creation," from the "Library Bill of Rights" was rewritten, "Secondary school librarians should not exclude materials because of the origin, background, or views of those contributing to their creation." During the pretesting process, the phrase "those contributing to their creation" was identified as confusing and was thus rewritten. The item became, "Secondary school librarians should not exclude materials because of the origin, background, or views of the author."

To measure censorship, items had to reflect the areas of restriction, or censorship, identified from the literature and experts as most common in school libraries. There are two points of restriction in school libraries: the first, in the decisions librarians make when selecting materials for purchase; and the second, in the decisions school librarians make about access to the resources in the library collection. Both types of restrictions had to be measured.

Three criteria were used to develop the censorship items. First, items had to reflect practices in school libraries. Second, items had to measure librarians' attitudes toward restrictive practices or censorship. And third, items had to discriminate among respondents who might have varying attitudes toward censorship. An example of the first criterion, an item reflecting school practices, is, "Some books should be marked 'for class use only' so they will be used with the guidance of a teacher." An example of an item reflecting the second criterion is, "Secondary school librarians should not select books that present our government in an unfavorable light." The third criterion was met by the provision of fixed alternative responses that allowed the expression of varying degrees of agreement or disagreement with the item. The use of the Likert scale—"strongly agree," "agree," "uncertain," "disagree," and "strongly disagree"—allowed discrimination among respondents who differed slightly.

DEVELOPMENT OF AN INSTRUMENT TO MEASURE INTELLECTUAL FREEDOM AND CENSORSHIP ATTITUDES

The first step in the process of developing the new instrument was to identify potential items. The item pool for the intellectual freedom portion of the test was developed by examining professional documents reflecting intellectual freedom beliefs. Statements of significance to school libraries were identified and reworded as needed to make them specific to school libraries. The item pool for the censorship portion of the test was developed using observation of current school library practices, the literature review, the Busha instrument, and expert opinion. Statements and remarks heard by the investigator over years of speaking about intellectual freedom to school librarian audiences provided items reflecting actual practices of school librarians. For example: "I agree with what you say, but my case is different. If my principal tells me to remove a book, I'll remove it." The item was stated: "If the principal requests that a book be removed from the secondary school library, the librarian should remove the book." Next, problem areas of current concern from the literature were identified. For example, the inclusion of resources representing a conservative point of view was identified as a current issue. Busha also included political publications as the object of three items. In the Busha instrument, an item referred to "right and left wing" publications. The item was, "A public library is no place for either right or left wing extremist political literature." Reflecting current terminology, the item was revised to refer to "liberal and conservative" publications: "A secondary school library is no place for either conservative or liberal extremist political literature." Busha's instrument included both right- and left-wing publications. For this study, one item was written: "Secondary school librarians should not purchase conservative publications such as *Moral Majority Newsletter* and *Conservative Digest.*" If the item were written now, *Conservative Chronicle* could be used to illustrate publications representing a conservative point of view.

Because self-censorship on the part of librarians is a sensitive subject, some of the items were written to allow the librarians to project the question to other people. Two items illustrate this projection. "Secondary school librarians should avoid purchasing books that might arouse local critics," and "Parents should be able to expect that the books in a secondary school library will not undermine their family values."

Category Descriptors

The next step in the development of the instrument was verification that the application items reflected professional beliefs, described restrictive practices, and represented the realm of these practices. Descriptors for the categories were written, following the methodology used by Getz (1985). The realm of restrictive practices was analyzed, and categories of practices identified and named. Categories were profession, policy, selection of resources, access to resources, diversity in collections, and controversial topics. The category names became the descriptors used in subsequent steps in the development of the instrument.

A prototype of the instrument containing eighty-five items and the six descriptors was developed, printed, and reviewed by two library professionals. These persons were selected because of their expertise in the area of intellectual freedom and research. Both of the experts had been recognized by their peers by being appointed to membership on American Library Association Intellectual Freedom committees. Both had written about intellectual freedom for national professional publications and both had frequently spoken about intellectual freedom to state and national audiences. One was an elected member of the Board of Trustees of the Freedom to Read Foundation and the other had been an appointed professional organization representative to that board. One of the persons was a retired professor of library science and the other a youth services librarian with degrees in both library science and young adult psychology. The latter degree included an emphasis on research methods.

Panel of Expert Judges

Following the review by these experts, the prototype was revised and prepared for review by a panel of expert judges. Items identified as unclear were modified, some items were eliminated, and one descriptor eliminated. At this point Controversy as a separate category was eliminated, and items moved to the Selection and Diversity categories. Items were then re-sorted by descriptor to reflect the revised list of restrictive practices. The items were also examined to detect duplication of content, and a count was made of the number of negatively stated and positively stated items for each descriptor. Ten items were eliminated at this point because of duplication of content. Additional items were eliminated because of lack of specificity. Seventy-two items and five descriptors remained. An instrument of seventy-two items was prepared for judges' ranking.

Thirty-five persons formed the judges' panel. The persons were intellectual freedom experts by virtue of service or professional position, e.g., service on intellectual freedom committees of professional associations, writings on intellectual freedom, recipients of intellectual freedom awards, and school library media educators known to have concerns about intellectual freedom. Thirty usable responses were returned. No follow-up reminder was sent. One response was returned as undeliverable and one response returned too late to be tabulated. These thirty responses were used to develop the *Intellectual Freedom/Censorship Attitude Scale.*

The judges examined the proposed instrument to: (1) assign a descriptor to each item, (2) determine the degree to which the item was descriptive of intellectual freedom or censorship, (3) identify neutral and unclear statements, and (4) identify essential missing concepts or practices. Items on

which there was disagreement about descriptors were eliminated, items identified as neutral were eliminated, and items
on which there was disagreement about the strength of the
description of intellectual freedom or censorship were eliminated. Unclear items were rewritten. No judge identified
missing concepts. Forty-four items were retained.

Pretesting the Attitude Scale

The forty-four-item instrument based on the opinions of
the judges was then pretested using the known-group
method, that is, persons belonging to a group of known
ideological persuasion (Crano and Brewer 1986: 51). The
pretest was administered to a group of national intellectual
freedom experts who had been called together by the Office
for Intellectual Freedom of the American Library Association
to design a method of gathering and reporting censorship
data. Each person attending the meeting was a representative
of an organization currently collecting, using, or publicizing
intellectual freedom and censorship information. No member of the population being studied was included in this
group. Five members of the group represented the library
community. Three were American Library Association staff:
one from the Office for Research and two from the Office for
Intellectual Freedom. Two persons represented types of
libraries. One represented school libraries and the other
person represented other types of libraries. Other groups
represented were the American Civil Liberties Union, National Coalition Against Censorship, National Council for the
Social Studies, National Council of Teachers of English, and
People for the American Way. The tests were administered
anonymously. Fourteen persons participated in the pretest.
One member of the group was a research consultant with no
professional expertise about intellectual freedom and censorship in schools. Because the research consultant was not a
member of the known group, his pretest (with his knowledge
and agreement) was not used in the item analysis.

The same instrument was administered to students in
library science classes at library schools in Michigan and

Missouri, states bordering the population states. One of the programs was accredited by the American Library Association (ALA) and the other was a college of education school library education program accredited by the National Council for the Accreditation of Teacher Education (NCATE). Students taking the pretest were enrolled in courses exclusively for school library media specialists. The geographical locations of the two universities where the pretest was administered provided certainty that subjects could not be commuting part-time students in the institutions. Further, since the pretests were administered during the school year, no member of the population to be surveyed was likely to be among the students taking the pretest.

Pretest Analysis

The results of the pretest were analyzed using the SPSSx test for reliability. Originally the *Statistical Package for the Social Sciences,* SPSSx is the trademark of a computer program used for computer analysis of data. The *Intellectual Freedom/ Censorship Attitude Scale* was found to be reliable. Cronbach's alpha index of internal consistency was .89 on the censorship portion of the pretest, .74 on the intellectual freedom portion of the pretest, and .90 on the combined pretest.

After pretesting and item analysis, an *Intellectual Freedom/ Censorship Attitude Scale* of thirty items was prepared. Ten intellectual freedom items were statements taken from professional documents, modified for school librarians. Twenty application items described restrictive practices. Because the purpose of an instrument measuring only intellectual freedom would have been obvious to respondents, as would an instrument measuring only restrictive practices, one test was developed to measure attitudes toward intellectual freedom and attitudes toward censorship. By interspersing intellectual freedom items with application, or censorship, items, the purpose of each item, or "right" answer might be less detectable. Items were arranged so that intellectual freedom items were separated from application items measuring the same concept. Some items were positively worded and some items were negatively worded. A five-point Likert scale was used. When data were analyzed, ratings were reversed for the negative items.

Validity and Reliability

During the development of the new instrument to measure attitudes toward intellectual freedom and censorship, care was taken to make the instrument as valid and reliable as possible. An instrument developed for a single study does not reach the levels of validity and reliability that an instrument would through repeated pretesting and use. However, major considerations and strategies recommended to ensure validity and reliability in the development of attitude survey instruments were identified and followed (Lemon 1973; Fishbein and Ajzen, 1975). No attempt was made to validate the instrument empirically. Rather, for the purposes of this study, the researcher relied on logical content validity. The test was not developed to predict behavior but to measure the degree to which respondents exhibited attitude agreement with intellectual freedom and censorship items.

Content validity. For the development of this instrument, content validity was assessed by the investigator's judgment and the opinions of intellectual freedom experts. Two factors were considered: the degree to which items represented professional attitudes and practices, and the scope of the practices described by the application items. The demands of content validity were met by the use of descriptors to provide a clear definition of the range of needed observations and the opinions of experts about the strength of the degree to which the items represented intellectual freedom and censorship.

Reliability. Cronbach's alpha index was used as a test of internal consistency. Following item analysis, the *Intellectual Freedom Attitude Scale* had an alpha of .8383, the *Censorship Attitude Scale* had an alpha of .9023, and the combined test .9251. Reliability coefficient ranges from .90 to 1.00 are defined as "excellent," and reliability coefficients ranging from .85 to .89 and .80 to .84 are defined as "very good" and "good," respectively. Balian (1982) suggested several conditions that tend to lower reliability coefficients, including short tests (fewer than twenty items) and attitudinal tests. Both conditions applied to the *Intellectual Freedom Attitude Scale.*

Interpretation of the Scores

The instrument designed to measure attitudes toward intellectual freedom and censorship consisted of thirty items. Ten items reflected attitudes toward professional values and beliefs, and twenty items reflected application of beliefs in practical terms, or descriptions of restrictive practices.

Intellectual Freedom/Censorship Attitude Scores. Attitudes were measured using a five-point Likert scale. Responses were scored using sums of responses and means. Overall a high score on the combined scale indicated agreement with intellectual freedom principles and a low score indicated a tendency to restrict access to information. A maximum score of 150 on the *Intellectual Freedom/Censorship Attitude Scale* indicated strong agreement with intellectual freedom principles and strong disagreement with restrictive practices.

Intellectual Freedom Attitude Scores. Ten items made up the intellectual freedom portion of the *Intellectual Freedom/ Censorship Attitude Scale.* The items were taken from the "Library Bill of Rights," interpretations of the "Library Bill of Rights," or the "Freedom to Read Statement," and were rewritten to indicate application to school librarians and school libraries. High scores indicated agreement with intellectual freedom principles as stated in professional documents. Low scores indicated disagreement with professional intellectual freedom statements. A maximum score of 50 indicated strong agreement with intellectual freedom principles.

Censorship Attitude Scores. Twenty application items made up the censorship portion of the test. These items reflected application of intellectual freedom principles in school library situations. High scores indicated disagreement with censorship or limiting access to information, while low scores indicated agreement with censorship or a tendency to restrict access to information. A maximum score of 100 reflected strong disagreement with restrictive practices.

MEASUREMENT OF MORAL JUDGMENT

Research in moral judgment has been conducted using two distinct measurement techniques. Both techniques use moral dilemma stories. One measurement technique is a moral judgment interview developed by Kohlberg and colleagues at Harvard in which the subject generates a solution to a moral dilemma. The other is an objectively scored, paper-and-pencil test developed by Rest at the University of Minnesota in which a subject rates and ranks a list of twelve issue statements on each of six stories involving moral dilemmas. A major difference between the two measurement techniques is the resulting score. Kohlberg's interview method results in a stage-specific score consistent with his view that individuals reside in a stage or in periods of transition between stages, partially in one stage and partially in the next stage. The *Defining Issues Test,* on the other hand, results in a Principled Moral Reasoning score (P score), which represents the amount of value a subject puts on principled moral reasoning when making decisions about a moral dilemma. The P score reflects Rest's belief that individuals do not reside in one stage, but that moral reasoning reflects a composite of factors that influence moral behavior or decision making.

Moral Judgment Interview

In Kohlberg's research at Harvard, scoring of moral judgment was based on an interview scheme in which subjects' responses to a series of questions about moral dilemma stories were analyzed. Scoring was based on sentence rating and global story ratings, essentially a content analysis (Colby and Kohlberg 1984: 42–43). The scoring method has gone through several revisions, resulting at times in a Moral Maturity Quotient, a Moral Judgment Score, and a Standard Stage Score. The Kohlberg scoring method has been criti-

cized as being time-consuming and expensive. Additionally,
the interview scoring method

> produces material that is not strictly comparable from
> subject to subject; the assessments are vulnerable to
> interviewer and scorer biases and scoring the material
> involves complex interpretations and rather great infer-
> ential leaps from the data. The test-retest reliability in
> several studies has been poor. . . . Correlations of
> Kohlberg's measure and similar scoring guides have
> been only moderate . . . [and] it is unclear to what extent
> differences in verbal expressiveness and other test-
> taking sets influence stage scores. (Rest 1975: 76–77)

Defining Issues Test

Early research on moral development used the Kohlberg
interview method, but since 1975 an objective paper-and-
pencil test has been available. Research on the *Defining Issues
Test (DIT)* "arose primarily in response to the need for a
practical, validated method for assessing moral judgment
and the need to establish a data base for the major claims of
the cognitive developmental theory" (Rest 1979: 14). Developed by James R. Rest of the University of Minnesota, the
Defining Issues Test has been successful in measuring "how
people choose the important issues of moral dilemmas." The
DIT results in a continuous P score, not a stage score. P scores
range from 00 to 95 and are "interpreted as the relative
importance a subject gives to morally principled considerations in making moral judgments." The *DIT* has been found
to be reliable (.81), and while not an equivalent test, shows
a correlation (.68) with Kohlberg's scale (Rest 1975: 76–80).
The validity of the *DIT* is based on four kinds of evidence:
longitudinal and cross-sectional data; consistency and stabil-
ity of subjects' scores over short periods of time; correlations with other psychological measures showing that the
DIT provides information beyond that accounted for by
the measure; and evidence that scores can be changed by
experimental treatment but not by manipulation, as when

subjects were instructed to " 'fake' good" answers (Rest 1986: xii).

Rest (1975: 77) described the methodological advantages of the *DIT* format:

> It is highly structured so that the information from each subject is comparable; it minimizes variance in stage scores caused by individual differences in verbal expressibility; it is objectively scored (can be computerized), saving time and minimizing scorer bias; and, because each test item and subject response is discrete and can be analyzed separately, each part of the test can be checked for reliability and its contribution to trends.

The *DIT,* however, cannot be administered to subjects with a reading level below twelve years and the multiple-choice format limits subjects' options to the twelve items representing possible ways of thinking.

From a study of the two measures of moral judgment, Alozie (1976) concluded that while a meaningful relationship existed between the *Moral Judgment Interview (MJI)* and the *DIT,* the homogeneity of the population determined the extent of the relationship. While both tests measured moral judgment development and both were derived from the same basic theoretical ideas about moral judgment, the *MJI* measured moral reasoning and the *DIT* measured the extent subjects understood and appreciated moral reasoning. Alozie concluded that the two tests were complementary. However, because the *DIT* is primarily a recognition test, and individuals are able to recognize moral reasoning before they are able to act in morally consistent ways, the *DIT* is likely to assign higher developmental stages to subjects.

MEASUREMENT OF MORAL REASONING

For reasons described above, an objectively scored paper-and-pencil test the (DIT) was selected to measure subjects' moral reasoning. While the identification of a test to measure moral reasoning was not a problem, two concerns were identified: (1) the need to administer two disparate, apparently unrelated instruments in the same survey; and (2) the length of the *DIT,* and consequently the time needed to complete it. The *DIT* was required by the research design, therefore efforts were made in the design of the questionnaire and in the letter of transmittal to minimize reluctance on the part of the potential respondents to complete the lengthy questionnaire.

Defining Issues Test

The *Defining Issues Test* consists of six stories describing moral situations and a series of twelve questions for each story. The subject rates the importance of each question as a consideration in making a decision about the situation. Subjects then identify and rank the four most important considerations. The ratings and rankings result in a P score, the amount of importance a subject gives to principled moral reasoning in responding to a moral dilemma. The twelve questions include items representing levels of moral reasoning and also items used to determine the usability of a subject's questionnaire. $\underline{A}$ items indicate an "antiestablishment" orientation, and $\underline{M}$ scores are "lofty sounding but meaningless" items. Questionnaires are rejected for using too many meaningless items. Inconsistencies between ratings and rankings also determine the usability of a subject's questionnaire.

Validity of the DIT. Rest (1979) described efforts to determine validity of the *DIT.* The *DIT* has been used in more than five hundred studies and has produced meaningful results. Therefore, Rest (1986: 179) concluded that the "DIT is a useful measure in moral judgment research." The *DIT* has been shown to be valid through criterion-group testing and longitudinal studies.

Reliability of the DIT. Rest, Davison, and Robbins (1978) reviewed studies using the *DIT* and found test-retest reliability to be in the high .70s and .80s. Rest (1986) reported internal consistency to be .77 and test-retest reliability to be .82.

Interpretation of P Score

The P score is the relative importance a subject gives to principled moral considerations in making a decision about moral dilemmas (Rest 1979: 101). Principled moral reasoning is indicated in Kohlberg's scheme as: Stage 5A, morality of social contract, Stage 5B, morality of intuitive humanism, and Stage 6, morality of principles of ideal social cooperation. P scores result from the sums of weighted ranks given to Stages 5 and 6 items. P scores are stated as percentages and range from 0 to 95 percent.

ARRANGEMENT OF QUESTIONNAIRE

The three-part questionnaire was labeled "School Library Issues and Social Problems." The first eleven questions asked for demographic information that had been identified from the literature review as likely to be significant. Included were questions about age, level of education, size of school, and membership in professional organizations. The second section of the questionnaire was labeled "School Library Issues" and included the thirty-item *Intellectual Freedom/Censorship Attitude Scale*. The third section, labeled "Opinions About Social Problems," included a page of directions and the six stories of the *Defining Issues Test*. Following the directions provided in the *Defining Issues Test* manual, no indication was given about the *DIT* being a measure of moral reasoning. Subjects were told that the survey "attempts to identify what school librarians/media specialists think about some current library issues and some general social problems."

Availability of Instruments

A copy of the *Intellectual Freedom/Censorship Attitude Scale* follows this chapter. The *Defining Issues Test* is included in a copy of the survey instrument in Appendix C. Permission to use the *Defining Issues Test* must be received from Dr. James R. Rest at the University of Minnesota. Detailed information about the *Defining Issues Test* is provided in *Moral Development: Advances in Research and Theory* (Rest 1986). Information about administering and scoring the *Defining Issues Test* is available in *The 1986 Manual for the DIT*. Copies may be obtained from

> The Center for the Study of Ethical Development
> University of Minnesota
> 206 Burton Hall
> 178 Pillsbury Drive S.E.
> Minneapolis, MN 55455

Anyone may use or adapt the *Intellectual Freedom/Censorship Attitude Scale*. Results of any research conducted using the instruments should be reported to Dr. Rest at the University of Minnesota and to Dr. McDonald at Box 20, Mankato State University, Mankato, MN 56002.

REFERENCES

Alozie, Chukwuma Francis Ethelbert. "An Analysis of the Interrelationship of Two Measures Used in the Measurement of Moral Judgment Development: The Kohlberg Moral Judgment Interview and the Rest Defining Issues Test." Doctoral dissertation, University of Minnesota, 1976.

Balian, Edward S. *How to Design, Analyze, and Write Doctoral Research: The Practical Guidebook*. Lanham, Maryland: University Press of America, 1982.

Busha, Charles H. "The Attitudes of Midwestern Public Librarians Toward Intellectual Freedom and Censorship." Doctoral dissertation, Indiana University, 1971.

Colby, Anne, and Lawrence Kohlberg. "Invariant Sequence and Internal Consistency in Moral Judgment Stages." In Kurtines, William M., and Jacob Gewirtz. *Morality, Moral Behavior, and Moral Development*. New York: John Wiley, 1984, 41–51.

Crano, William D., and Marilyn B. Brewer. *Principles and Methods of Social Research*. Boston: Allyn and Bacon, 1986.

Fishbein, Martin, and Icek Ajzen. *Belief, Attitude, Intention and Behavior*. Reading, Massachusetts: Addison-Wesley, 1975.

Getz, Irene Rose. "Moral Reasoning, Religion, and Attitudes Toward Human Rights." Doctoral dissertation, University of Minnesota, 1985.

Leedy, Paul D. *Practical Research: Planning and Design.* 3d ed. New York: Macmillan, 1985, 156.

Lemon, Nigel. *Attitudes and Their Measurement.* New York: John Wiley, 1973.

Rest, James R. *Development in Judging Moral Issues.* Minneapolis: University of Minnesota Press, 1979.

Rest, James R. *Moral Development: Advances in Research and Theory.* New York: Praeger, 1986.

Rest, James R. "Recent Research on an Objective Test of Moral Judgment: How the Important Issues of a Moral Dilemma Are Defined." In DePalma, David J., and Jeanne M. Foley. *Moral Development: Current Theory and Research.* Hillsdale, New Jersey: Lawrence Erlbaum, 1975, 75–93.

Rest, James R., Mark L. Davison, and Steven Robbins. "Age Trends in Judging Moral Issues: A Review of Cross-sectional, Longitudinal, and Sequential Studies of the Defining Issues Test." *Child Development* 49 (1978), 263–279.

Woodworth, Mary. *Intellectual Freedom, the Young Adult, and Schools: A Wisconsin Study.* Madison: University of Wisconsin, 1976.

INTELLECTUAL FREEDOM/CENSORSHIP ATTITUDE SCALE*

Please indicate your opinion of the following statements by circling the appropriate response.

SA   Strongly Agree
A   Agree
U   Uncertain
D   Disagree
SD   Strongly Disagree

12. The secondary school librarian's moral and aesthetic values should be the standard for determining what books should be included in the school library collection.   SA A U D SD

13. Some books should be marked "for class use only" so they will be used with the guidance of a teacher.   SA A U D SD

14. School librarians should be especially watchful to see that books containing unorthodox views are kept from secondary school library collections.   SA A U D SD

15. Secondary school librarians should avoid purchasing books that might arouse local critics.   SA A U D SD

16. Secondary school librarians should not exclude materials because of the origin, background, or views of the authors.   SA A U D SD

---

*Items 1 to 11 of the survey document ask for demographic information from respondents and are omitted here. The complete survey instrument is reproduced in Appendix C of this book; see pages 157–173.

17. Since secondary school librarians are in a position to recognize dangerous ideas in books and other printed materials, they should carefully control their circulation to students.   SA A U D SD

18. Secondary school librarians should avoid purchasing works of fiction dealing with social, psychological, and sexual problems and concentrate more on building collections of classics.   SA A U D SD

19. Secondary school librarians should not purchase conservative publications such as the *Moral Majority Newsletter* and *Conservative Digest.*   SA A U D SD

20. The procedure for dealing with challenged resources should be followed even if a teacher wants a book removed from the secondary school library.   SA A U D SD

21. Secondary school librarians should provide books and other materials presenting a variety of points of view on current and historic issues.   SA A U D SD

22. A censorship controversy over a single book or magazine is not worth the adverse publicity that it could cause for the school.   SA A U D SD

23. Secondary school students should have the freedom to read and consider a wider range of ideas than those that may be held by the majority in the community.   SA A U D SD

24. If the principal requests that a book be removed from the secondary   SA A U D SD

school library, the librarian should remove the book.

25. A secondary school library is no place for either conservative or liberal extremist political literature.   SA A U D SD

26. Books about controversial subjects should be starred as a guide for students who wish to avoid works of this type.   SA A U D SD

27. Secondary school librarians, as guardians of the students' freedom to read, should resist efforts of individuals or groups seeking to impose their views upon the school library.   SA A U D SD

28. Secondary school students need to have access to a variety of resources to help to develop critical thinking skills.   SA A U D SD

29. Controversial books in secondary school libraries should be kept on restricted shelves.   SA A U D SD

30. Secondary school librarians should be vigorous advocates of intellectual freedom.   SA A U D SD

31. If a secondary school librarian has ordered a controversial but positively reviewed book, and now the book is the object of court action in another school in the state, the librarian should cancel the order.   SA A U D SD

32. It is the responsibility of librarians to give full meaning to the freedom to read by providing books that enrich the quality of thought and expression.   SA A U D SD

33. Secondary school librarians should not purchase books which might offend the school principal.   SA A U D SD

34. Secondary school librarians should make it possible for students to choose freely from a variety of points of view on controversial subjects.   SA A U D SD

35. Secondary school librarians need not endorse every idea in the books they make available.   SA A U D SD

36. Secondary school librarians have a responsibility to see that school policies about selection and reevaluation of resources are followed.   SA A U D SD

37. Some issues, such as homosexuality, are just too controversial for a secondary school library.   SA A U D SD

38. Students should not use interlibrary loan to acquire books that the librarian has determined are not appropriate for the secondary school library collection.   SA A U D SD

39. Parents should be able to expect that the books in a secondary school library will not undermine their family values.   SA A U D SD

40. Secondary school librarians should make available the widest diversity of views and expressions, including those which are unpopular with the majority.   SA A U D SD

41. Secondary school librarians should not select books that present our government in an unfavorable light.   SA A U D SD

CHAPTER 6
DESCRIPTION OF SURVEY RESPONDENTS

The three-part survey was mailed to 450 randomly selected secondary school librarians in Iowa, Minnesota, and Wisconsin. School librarians returned 366 surveys, yielding a response rate of 81.33 percent. Thirty-eight incomplete or unusable surveys were eliminated, making a 72.88 percent response rate on which this research was based. Responses were divided almost equally among the three states.

Table 2

Responses

State	n	%
Iowa	107	32.6
Minnesota	110	33.5
Wisconsin	111	33.8

SIZE OF SCHOOL

The size of the schools in which the respondents worked ranged from small, with fewer than two hundred students, to large, with more than 1,000 students. Responses were almost equally divided between schools with fewer than 500 enrollment (47.9 percent) and more than 500 enrollment (52.1 percent). Only nine respondents (2.8 percent) reported school enrollments of more than 2,000 students, and twenty-one respondents reported school enrollments of fewer than

Table 3

Size of School

Size of School	Iowa n	%	Minnesota n	%	State Wisconsin n	%	Total n	%
0–199	9	(8.6)	6	(5.5)	6	(5.5)	21	(6.5)
200–299	17	(16.2)	14	(12.8)	10	(9.1)	41	(12.7)
300–499	33	(31.4)	24	(22.0)	36	(32.7)	93	(28.7)
500–999	23	(21.9)	31	(28.4)	31	(28.2)	85	(26.2)
1,000–1,999	21	(20.0)	29	(26.4)	25	(22.7)	75	(23.1)
2,000 or more	2	(1.9)	5	(4.6)	2	(1.8)	9	(2.8)

200 students. School enrollments in the three states were similar to the totals. Wisconsin closely paralleled the totals with 47.3 percent of the respondents reporting school enrollment of fewer than 500 students and 52.7 percent of the respondents reporting enrollment of more than 500 students. More Minnesota respondents reported large schools (59.4 percent) than Iowa or Wisconsin respondents, and more Iowa respondents reported small schools (56.2 percent) than the other two states.

Size of school rather than size of community was used as the measure of population because most school districts serve school-age children from a community along with the surrounding rural areas. Additionally, some school districts are consolidated, with one high school serving two or more communities. Consequently, size of school reflects only school population, not size of community in which the school was located. Previous researchers used size of community as a measure of population, so results are not comparable.

GRADES IN SCHOOL

In this study, secondary schools were defined as grades seven through twelve. One hundred forty-seven (44.8 percent) respondents reported working in senior high schools

Table 4

Grades in School

Grades	Iowa n	%	Minnesota n	%	Wisconsin n	%	Total n	%
7–8	8	(7.5)	4	(3.6)	0	(0.0)	12	(3.7)
7–9	7	(6.5)	10	(9.1)	0	(0.0)	17	(5.2)
7–12	31	(29.0)	30	(27.3)	25	(22.5)	86	(26.2)
9–12	29	(27.1)	18	(16.4)	62	(55.9)	109	(33.2)
10–12	15	(14.0)	13	(11.8)	10	(9.0)	38	(11.6)
Other[a]	15	(14.0)	32	(29.1)	12	(10.8)	59	(18.0)

[a]School included grades in addition to grades 7–12.

with grades nine through twelve, and thirty-eight (11.6 percent) in schools with grades ten through twelve. Twenty-nine respondents (8.9 percent) reported working in junior high schools. One-fourth (26.2 percent) of the respondents worked in grades seven through twelve schools. No Wisconsin respondent reported working in a school with only grades seven and eight or a school with only grades seven through nine, although twenty-five Wisconsin respondents reported working in schools with grades seven through twelve. Fifty-nine respondents (18 percent) reported working in schools including grades other than seven through twelve, or in elementary grades. Minnesota respondents reported the most schools with other grades (29.1 percent) compared with 14 percent in Iowa and 10.8 percent in Wisconsin.

AGE, GENDER, AND YEARS OF EXPERIENCE OF RESPONDENTS

Only ten (3.1 percent) of the respondents were under thirty, while two-thirds (217) of the respondents were forty or older. Fewer Minnesota respondents were under forty (20.5 percent) than Iowa (35.2 percent) or Wisconsin librarians (42.3). One hundred thirty-seven respondents (41.9 percent) reported having sixteen or more years experience. Thirty-six respondents reported having five or fewer years experience. Minnesota respondents were older and reported having had more years experience than either Iowa or Wisconsin respondents. While Minnesota and Wisconsin both had thirteen librarians with less than five years experience, 36 percent of Wisconsin librarians reported less than ten years experience compared with 26.6 percent in Minnesota. At the upper end of years of experience, almost half (48.6 percent) of Minnesota librarians had more than sixteen years experience, compared with 36 percent of Wisconsin subjects and 41.1 percent of Iowa respondents.

More than half (58.8 percent) of the respondents did not indicate sex when completing the questionnaire. Of those who answered the question, 97 (71.9 percent) were female

Table 5

Age of Respondents

Age	Iowa n	Iowa %	Minnesota n	Minnesota %	Wisconsin n	Wisconsin %	Total n	Total %
20–29	4	(3.8)	1	(0.9)	5	(4.5)	10	(3.1)
30–39	33	(31.4)	21	(19.6)	42	(37.8)	96	(29.7)
40–49	39	(37.1)	44	(41.1)	36	(32.4)	119	(36.8)
50–59	24	(22.9)	38	(35.5)	22	(19.8)	84	(26.0)
60 or over	5	(4.8)	3	(2.8)	6	(5.4)	14	(4.3)

Table 6

Years of Library Experience

Years	Iowa n	Iowa %	Minnesota n	Minnesota %	Wisconsin n	Wisconsin %	Total n	Total %
0–5	10	(9.3)	13	(11.9)	13	(11.7)	36	(11.0)
6–10	22	(20.6)	16	(14.7)	27	(24.3)	65	(19.9)
11–15	31	(29.0)	27	(24.8)	31	(27.9)	89	(27.2)
16–25	35	(32.7)	45	(41.3)	29	(26.1)	109	(33.3)
26 or more	9	(8.4)	8	(7.3)	11	(9.9)	28	(8.6)

Table 7

Gender of Respondents

Gender	Iowa n	%	Minnesota n	%	Wisconsin n	%	Total n	%
Male	12	(25.2)	15	(30.6)	11	(28.2)	38	(28.1)
Female	35	(74.5)	34	(69.4)	28	(71.8)	97	(71.9)

and 38 (28.1 percent) were male. The proportions were similar among the three states.

EDUCATION

Almost all respondents (96.9 percent) reported educational preparation beyond their first professional degrees. For most school librarians, the first professional degree is the baccalaureate leading to professional certification as a teacher. One hundred ninety (58.3 percent) of the respondents reported educational levels of a master's degree or more. Wisconsin respondents had the highest level of educational preparation with seventy-two librarians (64.8 percent) reporting master's degrees or more. Fifty-six (52.4 percent) of the Iowa librarians and 62 (57.4 percent) of Minnesota librarians reported educational preparation of a master's degree or more. Seven Minnesota respondents and two Iowa respondents reported specialist degrees.

Table 8

Level of Education

Education	Iowa n	%	Minnesota n	%	Wisconsin n	%	Total n	%
BA or BS	4	(3.7)	4	(3.7)	2	(1.8)	10	(3.1)
BA or BS plus	47	(43.9)	42	(38.9)	37	(33.3)	126	(38.7)
MA or MS	19	(17.8)	9	(8.3)	22	(19.8)	50	(15.3)
MA or MS plus	35	(32.7)	46	(42.6)	50	(45.0)	131	(40.2)
Specialist	2	(1.9)	7	(6.5)	0	(0.0)	9	(2.8)

Table 9

Institution of Professional Preparation

Institution	Iowa n %	Minnesota n %	Wisconsin n %
Private college	16 (15.0)	9 (8.3)	3 (2.7)
State university	77 (72.0)	97 (89.8)	84 (75.7)
ALA accredited	27 (25.2)	16 (14.8)	35 (31.5)

Subjects may have checked more than one option.

Most of the respondents (258) took courses for their professional licensure at state colleges or universities. Seventy-eight reported taking courses at an American Library Association accredited library school program. Only sixteen of the Minnesota respondents reported taking their courses at a library school program accredited by the American Library Association, compared with thirty-five Wisconsin respondents and twenty-seven Iowa respondents.

MEMBERSHIPS IN PROFESSIONAL ORGANIZATIONS

More than half of the respondents (57 percent) reported memberships in their state professional organizations. Most of the school librarians who were members of a state organization were members of the educational media organization rather than the state library association. Of those who were members of the state library association, Wisconsin respondents indicated more memberships (Wisconsin Library Association 26) than Minnesota (3) or Iowa (1) respondents. Wisconsin respondents also reported more state memberships (80) than Minnesota (62) or Iowa (69) respondents.

Only 43, or 13.1 percent, of the respondents reported memberships in national professional organizations. Most of these persons (36) were members of the American Library Association, and all but four of the American Library Association members were also members of the American Association of School Librarians. Perhaps related to the larger

Table 10

State Professional Organization Membership

State	Organization	n	%
Iowa	IEMA*	68	63.6[a]
	ILA	1	0.9
Minnesota	MEMO	59	53.6[b]
	MLA	3	2.7
Wisconsin	WEMA	54	48.6[c]
	WLA	26	23.4
Totals	Yes	187	57.0
	No	140	42.7

*IEMA–Iowa Educational Media Association
ILA–Iowa Library Association
MEMO–Minnesota Educational Media Organization
MLA–Minnesota Library Association
WEMA–Wisconsin Educational Media Association
WLA–Wisconsin Library Association

[a]Percent of Iowa respondents
[b]Percent of Minnesota respondents
[c]Percent of Wisconsin respondents

Table 11

National Professional Organization Membership

	ALA		AASL		AECT		DSMS	
State	n	%	n	%	n	%	n	%
Iowa	10	(9.3)	10	(9.3)	1	(0.9)	0	(0.0)[a]
Minnesota	9	(8.2)	8	(7.3)	2	(1.8)	2	(1.8)[b]
Wisconsin	17	(15.3)	14	(12.7)	3	(2.7)	2	(1.8)[c]
Totals	36	(11.0)	32	(9.8)	6	(1.8)	4	(1.2)

ALA–American Library Association
AASL–American Association of School Librarians (Must also be member of ALA)
AECT–Association for Educational Communications and Technology
DSMS–Division of School Media Specialists (Must also be member of AECT)

[a]Percent of Iowa respondents
[b]Percent of Minnesota respondents
[c]Percent of Wisconsin respondents

number of graduates from American Library Association accredited library school programs, Wisconsin respondents also indicated more memberships in the American Library Association (17) than Minnesota librarians (9) or Iowa librarians (10). Six respondents reported being members of the Association for Educational Communications and Technology and four of these persons reported being members of the school library division of that association—the Division of School Media Specialists. One respondent reported national membership, but did not identify the organization.

SUMMARY

Subjects in this study worked in grades seven through twelve schools. The sample was almost equally divided between school librarians working in schools with more than 500 students and those with fewer than 500 students. Most respondents were experienced, with only 36 reporting five or fewer years working as a school librarian. Experience was reflected in the age of the respondents, with most reporting being forty or older. Subjects were highly educated: most had earned master's degrees and had attended a state college or university for their professional preparation. More than half of the respondents were members of their state professional organizations, but fewer than 15 percent were members of national professional organizations.

A profile of the typical respondent can be constructed. The school librarian is a female over forty years old, with more than ten years experience. She has earned a master's degree from a state college or university. She is a school librarian in a high school with grades nine through twelve and is as likely to be working in a large school as a smaller school. She is a member of her state professional media organization, but not a member of a national professional organization.

CHAPTER 7
INTELLECTUAL FREEDOM AND CENSORSHIP ATTITUDES AND DEMOGRAPHIC CHARACTERISTICS

Based on the results of previous researchers, significant differences related to demographic characteristics were expected. Not all results reported here support previous findings, although trends were observed. In previous studies, size of community was found to be significantly related to attitudes toward intellectual freedom and censorship. In this study, size of school was significantly related to attitudes toward intellectual freedom and censorship. Level of education has consistently been found to be related to attitudes toward intellectual freedom and censorship, and the findings were replicated in this study. Previous findings related to gender were not supported in this study.

Two null hypotheses were tested:

There are no significant relationships among variables such as size of school, geographical location of school district, grade levels in school, age, sex, and educational level of secondary school librarians and their attitudes toward intellectual freedom as measured by the *Intellectual Freedom/Censorship Attitude Scale*.

There are no significant relationships among variables such as size of school, geographical location of school district, grade levels in school, age, sex, and educational level of secondary school librarians and their attitudes toward censorship as measured by the *Intellectual Freedom/Censorship Attitude Scale*.

The first null hypothesis was rejected in part. Size of school (f ratio 4.8399, p <.0003) and level of education (f ratio 9.0747, p <.0000) were found to be significantly related to intellectual freedom attitudes. No significant differences were found among intellectual freedom attitude scores and geographical location of subject (f ratio .8924, p =.4107), grade levels in school (f ratio 1.8046, p =.1115), age (f ratio .8021, p =.5245), or gender (t value .13, p =.895).

The second null hypothesis was also rejected in part. Censorship attitudes were significantly related to size of school (f ratio 6.7526, p <.0000), grade levels in school (f ratio 2.9879, p <.0119), and level of education (f ratio 9.3611, p <.0000) of school librarians, but not to geographical location (f ratio 2.4805, p =.0853), age (f ratio 1.0663, p =.3733), or gender of librarians (t value .45, p =.653).

SIZE OF SCHOOL

An analysis of variance showed significant differences (f ratio 4.8399, p =.0003) among subjects and size of school on the *Intellectual Freedom Attitude Scale*. Subjects from schools with enrollments from 1,000 to 1,999 had significantly higher scores on the *Intellectual Freedom Attitude Scale* than subjects from smaller schools, that is, schools with enrollments of fewer than 500 students. Librarians in smaller schools were less likely to agree with intellectual freedom principles than librarians in larger schools.

Size of school was also significantly related to scores on the *Censorship Attitude Scale*. Subjects who worked in schools of 500–999 enrollment were significantly different from subjects who worked in the smallest schools of fewer than 200 students (f ratio 6.7526, p <.0000). Subjects who worked in schools with 1,000–1,999 enrollment also had significantly higher scores than librarians who worked in schools with fewer than 500 enrolled.

Table 12

Intellectual Freedom and Censorship Attitude
Scores and Size of School

Size of school	n	IF$\bar{x}$	sd	C$\bar{x}$	sd
–199	21	42.5714*	3.9188	75.6190*	10.5474
200–299	41	43.4390*	3.6814	78.3659*	10.3580
300–499	93	43.3656*	4.7038	81.1429*	9.8495
500–999	85	44.6235	4.1374	82.0238*	9.6267
1,000–1,999	75	45.9067*	3.3295	86.8767*	9.4618
2,000 and more	9	45.8889	3.6553	83.3333	7.2629
Totals	324	44.3117	4.1822	82.0282	10.1904

*p <.05

GEOGRAPHICAL LOCATION OF SCHOOL DISTRICT

Subjects from all three states had similar scores on the *Intellectual Freedom/Censorship Attitude Scale* resulting in no significant differences among respondents on either scale (intellectual freedom attitudes: f ratio .8924, p =.4107, and censorship attitudes: f ratio 2.4805, p =.0853). Although no statistically significant differences were found among the three states, slight differences in mean scores appeared. The mean can be described as the average score that is calculated by dividing the sum of all the scores by the number of scores. Iowa respondents showed the lowest means on both the *Censorship* and *Intellectual Freedom Attitude Scales,* and Wisconsin respondents had the highest means on both scales.

GRADE LEVELS IN SCHOOL

Although not significant, the subjects in schools with grades seven, eight, and nine showed less agreement with intellectual freedom principles than subjects in schools with

Table 13

Intellectual Freedom and Censorship Attitude Scores
Means and Standard Deviations on Attitude Scales
and Geographical Location of Subjects

| | | Attitude Scale | |
State	Intellectual Freedom	Censorship	Combined
Iowa			
Mean	43.907	80.343	124.305
Standard deviation	4.253	9.615	12.896
Minnesota			
Mean	44.364	82.477	126.862
Standard deviation	4.223	11.448	14.695
Wisconsin			
Mean	44.658	83.349	127.991
Standard deviation	4.058	9.177	12.422
All subjects			
Mean	44.314	82.077	126.412
Standard deviation	4.176	10.180	13.426

Table 14

Intellectual Freedom and Censorship
Attitude Scores and Grade Levels in School

Grades	n	IF$\bar{x}$	sd	C$\bar{x}$	sd
7–8	12	43.7500	3.7929	81.5000	6.9216
7–9	17	43.4706	4.4175	81.1176	10.9481
7–12	86	44.7442	4.1620	80.0930*	10.7579
9–12	109	44.6147	4.1207	83.2617	9.8386
10–12	38	45.0789	4.2641	86.8611*	7.9216
Other[a]	66	43.1364	4.2641	80.4615*	10.5550
Total	328	44.3140	4.1096	82.0774	10.1802

* $p < .05$
[a] Other: schools with grades in addition to 7 - 12.

Table 15

Intellectual Freedom and Censorship
Attitude Scores and Years of Experience

Experience	n	IF$\bar{x}$	sd	C$\bar{x}$	sd
0–5	36	44.3056	3.9484	79.4571	10.2766
6–10	65	43.3692	4.5400	81.4308	9.5590
11–15	89	44.8539	3.6852	83.1932	10.0709
16–25	109	44.7339	4.1648	83.0755	10.1105
over 25	28	42.9643	4.6466	79.1071	11.3508
Total	327	44.2966	4.1705	82.0373	10.1704

grades ten through twelve. Subjects in grades seven and eight schools had a mean of 43.7500, subjects in schools with grades seven through nine had a mean of 43.4706, and subjects in schools with other grades had a mean of 43.1364, while subjects in schools with grades ten through twelve had a mean of 45.0789.

On the *Censorship Attitude Scale,* significant differences were observed (f ratio 2.9879, p <.0119). Subjects who worked in schools with grades ten through twelve were significantly different ($\bar{x}$ = 86.8611) from subjects from schools with grades seven through twelve ($\bar{x}$ = 80.093) and schools with other grades ($\bar{x}$ = 80.4615), but not with subjects from schools with grades seven and eight or seven through nine.

YEARS OF EXPERIENCE

No significant differences were observed on the *Intellectual Freedom Attitude Scale* (f ratio 2.2489, p =.0637) or on the *Censorship Attitude Scale* (f ratio 1.7794, p =.1327) related to years of experience. Of interest, however, is that librarians with the least experience ($\bar{x}$ = 79.4571) and librarians with the most experience ($\bar{x}$ = 79.1071) had the lowest means on the *Censorship Attitude Scale.* Although experience was not found to be statistically significant on either scale in this study, previous researchers had found significance. Pope (1974) found that librarians with fewer years experience were less restrictive than librarians with more years experience. Farley (1964) also found that librarians with more than twenty-five years experience were more restrictive than librarians with fewer years experience.

AGE AND GENDER OF RESPONDENTS

No differences were observed based on age or gender on the *Intellectual Freedom Attitude Scale* or the *Censorship Attitude Scale.* However, subjects in the youngest ($\bar{x} = 43.80$) and oldest ($\bar{x} = 43.5429$) age categories showed the lowest mean scores on the *Intellectual Freedom Attitude Scale* and on the *Censorship Attitude Scale* ($\bar{x} = 78.50$ and $\bar{x} = 77.9231$). Busha (1971) also found a slight increase in restrictiveness with increases in age, though not at a significant level.

Female librarians had lower mean scores on both attitude scales, although not at a level of significance. In previous studies, both Busha (1971) and Pope (1974) found that female librarians were more likely than male librarians to hold

Table 16

Intellectual Freedom and Censorship
Attitude Scores and Age

Age	n	IF$\bar{x}$	sd	C$\bar{x}$	sd
20–29	10	43.8000	4.3410	78.5000	11.0378
30–39	96	44.0938	4.1954	82.2000	8.9474
40–49	119	44.8655	4.0083	82.9328	11.2066
50–59	84	44.0357	4.3918	82.0617	9.6389
60 +	14	43.6429	4.1990	77.9231	10.6572
Total	323	44.3344	4.1792	82.1478	10.1528

Table 17

Intellectual Freedom and Censorship
Attitude Scores and Gender

Gender	n	IF$\bar{x}$	s.d.	C$\bar{x}$	sd
Male	38	44.2895	4.730	81.7632	10.050
Female	97	44.1856	3.858	80.8172	11.236

restrictive attitudes. No significant differences were found in this study, although trends supporting the Busha and Pope findings were observed.

LEVEL OF EDUCATION

Educational preparation was found to be the most significant variable in this study. Scores of respondents with master's degrees or with master's degrees plus additional credits were significantly different from scores of respondents with bachelor's degrees plus additional credits on both the *Intellectual Freedom Attitude Scale* and the *Censorship Attitude Scale* (Intellectual Freedom f ratio 9.0747, p <.0000, and Censorship f ratio 9.3611, p <.0000). This finding indicated that librarians with educational preparation of a master's degree or more held more positive attitudes toward intellectual freedom and were less restrictive than librarians with bachelor's degrees plus additional credits.

The findings in this study supported previous research. Pope (1974: 165) also found that librarians with higher levels of education were less restrictive than librarians with less educational preparation. Busha (1971) found significant differences between level of education and intellectual freedom and censorship attitudes, and considered level of education to be the single most significant variable accounting for differ-

Table 18

Intellectual Freedom and Censorship
Attitude Scores and Level of Education

Level of Education	n	IF$\bar{x}$	s.d.	C$\bar{x}$	sd
BA,BS	10	44.5000	3.6286	81.0000	11.7094
BA,BS +	126	42.8016*	4.2351	78.1129*	9.9423
MA,MS	50	44.4400*	4.2960	83.4400*	11.6271
MA,MS +	131	45.7786*	3.5633	85.4219*	8.3483
Specialist	9	44.6667	4.0927	83.5556	9.4089
Total	326	44.3528	4.1586	82.0997	10.1675

*p <.05

ences in attitudes toward intellectual freedom and censorship among public librarians.

INTELLECTUAL FREEDOM AND CENSORSHIP AND MEMBERSHIP IN STATE AND NATIONAL PROFESSIONAL ORGANIZATIONS

Two null hypotheses were tested:

There is no significant relationship between membership in state and national professional organizations and the attitudes of secondary school librarians toward intellectual freedom as measured by the *Intellectual Freedom/Censorship Attitude Scale.*

There is no significant relationship between membership in state and national professional organizations and the attitudes of secondary school librarians toward censorship as measured by the *Intellectual Freedom/ Censorship Attitude Scale.*

Both null hypotheses were rejected. Membership in state and national professional organizations contributed significantly to scores on the *Intellectual Freedom Attitude Scale* and to scores on the *Censorship Attitude Scale*. Members of professional organizations had higher means on both scales. Although the number of subjects was small, memberships in the American Library Association and American Association of School Librarians were significantly related to intellectual freedom and censorship attitudes, but memberships in the Association of Educational Communications and Technology and Division of School Media Specialists were not significant.

Table 19

Intellectual Freedom Attitude Scores and National Memberships

Member	n	x̄	s.d.	t value	d.f.	prob.
ALA						
yes	36	46.0833	3.459	−2.66	318	.008
no	284	44.1338	4.224			
AASL						
yes	32	46.0938	3.344	−2.50	318	.013
no	288	44.1597	4.230			
AECT						
yes	6	45.6667	3.445	−.78	318	.439
no	314	44.3280	4.199			
DSMS						
yes	4	45.7500	2.500	−.67	318	.503
no	316	44.3354	4.202			
Total						
yes	43	46.0000	3.374	2.81	319	.005
no	278	44.0971	4.239			

ALA American Library Association
AASL American Association of School Librarians
AECT Association for Educational Communications and Technology
DSMS Division of School Media Specialists

Table 20

Censorship Attitude Scores and National Memberships

Member	n	x̄	s.d.	t value	d.f.	prob.
ALA						
yes	36	86.2778	10.047	−2.57	313	.011
no	279	81.6631	10.170			
AASL						
yes	32	87.5000	7.812	−3.14	313	.002
no	283	81.5901	10.326			
AECT						
yes	6	88.1667	6.242	−1.44	313	.149
no	309	82.0744	10.281			
DSMS						
yes	4	91.2500	1.708	−1.79	313	.075
no	311	82.0740	10.259			
Total						
yes	43	86.1395	9.443	2.76	314	.006
no	273	81.5604	10.227			

ALA American Library Association
AASL American Association of School Librarians
AECT Association for Educational Communications and Technology
DSMS Division of School Media Specialists

Although not statistically significant in every case on the state level, the means of organization members on both scales and in all organizations were higher than the means of librarians who were not members of professional organizations. Only Iowa respondents who reported being members of IEMA had scores that reached a significant level (Intellectual Freedom t value 2.18, p = .032, and Censorship t value 3.60, p <.000). Fiske (1959) found that memberships in professional organizations correlated with school librarians in the middle category, that is, neither highly restrictive nor

Table 21

Intellectual Freedom Attitude Scores and State Memberships

Member		n	x̄	s.d.	t value	d.f.	prob.
IEMA	No	39	42.7436	4.259	−2.18	105	.032
	Yes	68	44.5735	4.133			
ILA*							
MEMO	No	50	44.1000	4.478	−.69	107	.492
	Yes	59	44.6610	4.011			
MLA*							
WEMA	No	57	44.0877	4.469	−1.53	109	.129
	Yes	54	45.2593	3.514			
WLA	No	85	44.3529	4.119	−1.44	109	.153
	Yes	26	45.6538	3.752			
All subjects	Yes	187	44.7861	3.922	2.31	324	.021
	No	140	43.7143	4.432			

IEMA–Iowa Educational Media Association
ILA–Iowa Library Association
MEMO–Minnesota Educational Media Organization
MLA–Minnesota Library Association
WEMA–Wisconsin Educational Media Association
WLA–Wisconsin Library Association

*Numbers were too small to produce meaningful results.
Iowa (1) Minnesota (3).

highly permissive. Fiske concluded that memberships in professional organizations contributed to more restrictive attitudes among school librarians, a finding not replicated in this
study. Fiske observed that nonmembers tended not to take
controversy into account when making selection decisions.

UNHYPOTHESIZED FINDINGS

The significant relationship between the institution of
educational preparation and intellectual freedom attitudes

Table 22

Censorship Attitude Scores and State Memberships

Member		n	x̄	s.d.	t value	d.f.	prob.
IEMA	No	39	76.1795	9.486	−3.60	103	.000
	Yes	66	82.8030	8.874			
ILA*							
MEMO	No	50	81.2400	11.061	−1.10	106	.274
	Yes	58	83.6724	11.805			
MLA*							
WEMA	No	57	81.9825	8.450	−1.64	107	.104
	Yes	52	84.8462	9.775			
WLA	No	83	82.9880	9.609	−.73	106	.466
	Yes	26	84.5000	7.690			
All subjects	Yes	182	83.4725	9.967	2.79	320	.006
	No	140	80.3143	10.232			

IEMA–Iowa Educational Media Association
ILA–Iowa Library Association
MEMO–Minnesota Educational Media Organization
MLA–Minnesota Library Association
WEMA–Wisconsin Educational Media Association
WLA–Wisconsin Library Association

*Numbers were too small to produce meaningful results.
Iowa (1) Minnesota (4).

and censorship attitudes was an unexpected finding. Subjects who attended library school programs accredited by the American Library Association scored higher on both the *Intellectual Freedom Attitude Scale* (f ratio 4.8581, p = .0083) and the *Censorship Attitude Scale* (f ratio 3.6983, p = .0259) than subjects from other state colleges and universities and private colleges. The results of t-tests comparing subjects from ALA library school programs and subjects from other state colleges and universities and private schools combined further illustrated differences based on institution of educational preparation (Intellec-

Table 23

Intellectual Freedom and Censorship
Attitude Scores and Institution of
Educational Preparation

Institution	n	x̄	s.d.	t value	d.f.	prob.
Intellectual Freedom Score						
ALA	80	45.5500	3.835	3.08	326	.002
Other	248	42.9153	4.211			
Censorship Score						
ALA	78	84.2308	10.225	2.16	321	.032
Other	245	81.3918	10.091			
Combined Score						
ALA	78	129.8333	13.432	2.61	321	.010
Other	245	125.3224	13.267			

ALA Library School program accredited by the American Library Association
Other Other institutions of educational preparation

tual Freedom t value 3.08, p = .002, and Censorship
t value 2.16, p = .032). No other researcher investigated
institution of educational preparation, so no comparisons
are possible.

After the completion of the original research, further
analysis was conducted to determine whether the differences
between subjects from ALA accredited programs and subjects from other programs could be explained by level of
education. Because subjects from ALA programs were likely
to hold master's degrees, found to be significant in explaining differences in means scores on all attitude scales, additional t-tests were run using only subjects with master's
degrees or with master's degrees and additional credits.
The results reported in Table 24 show that differences
between subjects on agreement with the principles of intellectual freedom could be explained by institution of educational preparation, but not differences in application of the
principles. Subjects from ALA programs showed significantly
different mean scores on the *Intellectual Freedom Attitude Scale*
(p = .052), but no significant differences were observed on

Table 24

Intellectual Freedom and Censorship Attitude Scores,
Institution of Educational Preparation,
and Master's Degrees

Institution	n	x̄	s.d.	t value	d.f.	prob.
Intellectual Freedom Score						
ALA MS degree	76	46.0395	3.368	1.96	198	.052
Other MS degree	124	44.9677	3.979			
Censorship Score						
ALA MS degree	68	85.6765	9.051	1.00	186	.317
Other MS degree	120	84.2500	9.530			
Combined Score						
ALA MS degree	68	131.8529	11.699	1.40	185	.164
Other MS degree	119	129.2437	12.157			

ALA Library school program accredited by the American Library Association
Other Other institutions of educational preparation

the *Censorship Attitude Scale* (p = .317) or on the combined scale (p = .164).

SUMMARY

Intellectual freedom attitudes were found to be significantly related to level of education, size of school, professional memberships, and institution of educational preparation. Censorship attitudes were found to be significantly related to level of education, size of school, grade levels in school, professional memberships, and institution of educational preparation. Educational preparation was found to be the most significant variable in explaining differences in mean scores on all attitude scales. Geographical location of subjects, age, years of experience, and gender showed no significant relationships on either scale.

REFERENCES

Busha, Charles H. "The Attitudes of Midwestern Public Librarians Toward Intellectual Freedom and Censorship." Doctoral dissertation, Indiana University, 1971.

Farley, John J. "Book Censorship in the Senior High Libraries of Nassau County, New York." Doctoral dissertation, New York University, 1964.

Fiske, Marjorie (Lowenthal). *Book Selection and Censorship: A Study of School and Public Librarians in California.* Berkeley: University of California Press, 1959.

Pope, Michael. *Sex and the Undecided Librarian: A Study of Librarians' Opinions on Sexually Oriented Literature.* Metuchen, New Jersey: Scarecrow Press, 1974.

CHAPTER 8
INTELLECTUAL FREEDOM
AND CENSORSHIP
CONSISTENCY

Lack of consistency between the expression of professional beliefs and application of the principles exhibited by librarians is no longer a surprise. Evidence from research reports as early as 1959, and replicated in virtually every study since, indicates that school librarians voice agreement with the principles of their profession, but are not always in agreement with the application of the principles. Professional behavior also indicates that while school librarians appear to know the major tenets in professional documents, they do not always apply the principles in actual practice and, at times, freely admit removing or restricting resources for reasons unrelated to the purposes of the school library.

The results of this study provided further evidence of inconsistencies in attitudes of secondary school librarians in Iowa, Minnesota, and Wisconsin toward intellectual freedom and censorship. As expected, school librarians expressed strong agreement with the principles of their profession, but were less likely to agree with application of the principles. An unexpected finding was the degree of use of the "uncertain" option in responding to application items. Perhaps reflecting reluctance to disagree with application of known principles, perhaps reflecting actual behavior, a relatively large number of respondents chose the "uncertain" option when responding to application items.

INTELLECTUAL FREEDOM AND CENSORSHIP

The null hypothesis was:

> There is no significant relationship between the attitudes of secondary school librarians toward intellectual freedom and their attitudes toward censorship as measured by the *Intellectual Freedom/Censorship Attitude Scale.*

The null hypothesis was rejected. High significant correlations were found between intellectual freedom scores and censorship scores ($r = .6937$, $p < .001$). Subjects who scored high on the *Intellectual Freedom Attitude Scale* tended to score high on the *Censorship Attitude Scale,* indicating agreement with both the principles of intellectual freedom and the application of those principles. Busha (1971) also found a statistically significant correlation ($r = .60$, $p < .01$) between intellectual freedom attitudes and censorship attitudes in his study of public librarians.

If attitudes toward intellectual freedom were absolutely related to attitudes toward censorship, a correlation of 1.00 would have been observed. Correlations of the magnitude observed in this study accounted for 48 percent of the variance in the scores.

For descriptive purposes, scores were grouped to illustrate numbers of high- and low-scoring subjects. High-scoring sub-

Table 25

Correlations Among Intellectual Freedom Scores, Censorship Scores, and Combined Scores

	IF Scores	C Scores	IF/C Scores
IF Scores	1.000	.6937**	.8377**
C Scores		1.0000	.9745**
IF/C Scores			1.0000

n = 323
** p < .001

jects were more than one standard deviation above the mean, and low-scoring subjects were more than one standard deviation below the mean. In a normal distribution, two-thirds of the scores are expected to fall within one standard deviation above and below the mean. These categories were used for descriptive purposes only, not for hypotheses testing.

Results indicated that all subjects generally agreed with intellectual freedom principles, since no intellectual freedom score was lower than 34 (possible score 50). Seventy-one subjects scored high (49 or 50) on the *Intellectual Freedom Attitude Scale,* and 45 subjects scored low (34 to 40). High intellectual freedom scores indicated strong agreement with intellectual freedom principles. Illustrating the expected lower agreement with application items, 45 subjects scored high (92–100) on the *Censorship Attitude Scale* compared with 52 (50–71) low-scoring subjects (possible score 100). Low scores on the *Censorship Attitude Scale* indicated a tendency to restrict access to the resources made available to students, or to be restrictive in selecting resources. High scores on the *Censorship Attitude Scale* indicated disagreement with restricting access to resources. Subjects with scores in the middle range could be described as neither strongly agreeing with applying intellectual freedom principles nor strongly restrictive in applying the principles.

Table 26

Intellectual Freedom/Censorship Attitude Scale
Grouped Scores of All Subjects

	IF Scores		C Scores	
	n	range	n	range
High	71	49–50	45	92–100
Middle	207	41–48	226	72–91
Low	45	34–40	52	50–71
Totals	323	34–50	323	50–100
(Possible range		10–50		20–100)

Combining scores provided another look at consistency between attitudes toward intellectual freedom and attitudes toward censorship. Only 39 respondents (12.1 percent) strongly agreed with intellectual freedom principles and also strongly disagreed with restrictive practices. Twenty-four subjects scored low on both the *Intellectual Freedom Attitude Scale* and the *Censorship Attitude Scale,* indicating disagreement with intellectual freedom principles and agreement with restrictive practices. No subjects with low scores on the *Intellectual Freedom Attitude Scale* scored high on the *Censorship Attitude Scale.* However, illustrating inconsistency, two subjects with high intellectual freedom scores scored low on the *Censorship Attitude Scale,* illustrating strong agreement with intellectual freedom principles, but also strong agreement with restrictive practices.

The findings in this study can be compared with Farley's

Table 27

High, Middle, or Low Intellectual Freedom Attitude Scores
and High, Middle, or Low Censorship Attitude Scores

Intellectual Freedom Score	Censorship Score			
	Low (50–71)	Middle (72–91)	High (92–100)	Total
Low	24	21	0	45
(34–40)	7.4%	6.5%	0.0%	13.9%
Middle	19	175	13	207
(41–48)	5.9%	54.2%	4.0%	64.1%
High	2	30	39	71
(49–50)	0.6%	9.3%	12.1%	22.0%
Total for Each Group	45 13.9%	226 70.0%	52 16.1%	
Grand Total				323 100%

(High Intellectual Freedom scores indicated agreement with intellectual freedom principles. Low Censorship scores indicated agreement with restrictive application of intellectual freedom principles.)

1964 study of school librarians and Busha's 1971 study of public librarians. While differences in methodology preclude exact comparisons, some observations can be made about the findings. Busha used standard deviations to categorize his subjects, while Farley assigned his subjects to categories representing restrictive or permissive attitudes with the remainder of the librarians assigned to the middle category. Both Busha and Farley found results similar to those reported here in the middle range. Fifty-five percent of Busha's subjects showed middle-range scores, and 55.5 percent of Farley's subjects were assigned to the middle range, compared with 54.2 percent of the subjects in this study. Although middle scores were almost the same, high and low scores were different. More of Busha's subjects (18.2 percent) had low intellectual freedom scores than the 13.9 percent here, and fewer (12.2 percent) of Busha's subjects had high intellectual freedom scores than the 22 percent scoring high in this study. More of the school librarians in this study agreed with intellectual freedom principles than the public librarians in Busha's study.

Farley found that 11 percent of the librarians in his study exhibited restrictive attitudes, compared with 13.9 percent of the librarians in this study. While 33 percent of Farley's subjects were considered permissive (that is, disagreeing with restrictive practices), 16.1 percent of the subjects here disagreed with restrictive practices. In other words, twice as many of Farley's subjects disagreed with restrictive practices as subjects reported here disagreed with restrictive practices.

CONSISTENCY BETWEEN INTELLECTUAL FREEDOM ITEMS AND APPLICATION ITEMS

Arranging intellectual freedom items and application items by descriptor illustrated consistency among intellectual freedom items and application items measuring the same concept. It was expected that some inconsistency would be observed. Subjects would agree with intellectual freedom items, but not agree so strongly with application items. Inconsistencies were observed in all categories of descriptors. To aid in comprehending overall agreement or disagreement, "strongly agree" responses and "agree" responses were combined and considered "agree." Similarly, "disagree" and "strongly disagree" responses were grouped and considered "disagree." The combining was used to group similar scores for descriptive purposes only. Scores were assigned their numerical value for analysis of the data. Exact frequencies are provided in Appendix D.

Policy

The items under the policy descriptor illustrated the professional responsibility of librarians to monitor school policies about access to resources and the positive stance of the librarians in support of intellectual freedom principles. Application items illustrated librarians carrying out these responsibilities.

Although advocacy of intellectual freedom is one of the primary principles of the profession, 23 respondents to this study were uncertain or disagreed with that role. Only 4 respondents were uncertain and no one disagreed that secondary school librarians have a responsibility to see that policies about selection and reevaluation of resources were followed. However, differences appeared when school librarians were asked to respond to application items. If a teacher wanted a book removed, 96.9 percent of the school librarians agreed that policies should be followed. But if a principal wanted to remove a book, 12.8 percent disagreed with following the policy and 14.9 percent were uncertain. These findings were similar to those of Fiske (1959) and Douma (1976), who both found that requests to restrict information from within the school were more likely to be successful than requests from persons outside the school. Further, Fiske found that librarians working for restrictive principals tended to be restrictive. Even more descriptive of attitudes was the finding that 101 of the respondents (30.7 percent) agreed or were uncertain about whether a censorship controversy was worth the adverse publicity it could cause the school. This finding is not altogether surprising, however. Librarians have frequently been heard to explain that their reluctance to resist

Table 28

Intellectual Freedom and Censorship Attitudes:
Means and Frequencies
Policy Category

	x̄	s.d.		f	%
Intellectual Freedom Items					
30. Secondary school librarians should be vigorous advocates of intellectual freedom.	4.424	0.677	a* u* d*	305 17 6	93.0 5.2 1.8
36. Secondary school librarians have a responsibility to see that school policies about selection and reevaluation of resources are followed.	4.537	0.523	a u d	324 4 0	98.9 1.2 0.0
Application Items					
20. The procedure for dealing with challenged resources should be followed even if a teacher wants a book removed from the secondary school library.	4.450	0.634	a u d	317 7 3	96.9 2.1 .9
22. A censorship controversy over a single book or magazine is not worth the adverse publicity that it could cause for the school.	3.854	0.972	a u d	33 68 227	10.0 20.7 69.2
24. If the principal requests that a book be removed from the secondary school library, the library should remove the book.	3.881	0.987	a u d	42 49 237	12.8 14.9 72.3

*a   agree
*u   uncertain
*d   disagree

removing resources is related to pending bond issues or contract negotiations. Librarians also report that colleagues pressure them to remove challenged resources rather than incur negative publicity for the school district.

Of interest was the number of librarians who were uncertain about their responses. While few respondents used the "uncertain" category when considering the intellectual freedom item referring to the librarian's responsibility to see that policies were followed, 49 respondents selected "uncertain" when administrators were the focus of the application item. This finding further illustrated the influence of school administrators and the ambivalence of librarians about that influence. The number of respondents (68) who selected the "uncertain" option for the item referring to the possible adverse publicity a censorship incident could cause also illustrated ambivalent attitudes toward applying the principles of intellectual freedom.

Diversity

The diversity category included items about providing resources representing a variety of points of view, including ideas with which the librarian or community might disagree.

Almost all of the respondents (98.7 percent) recognized that librarians did not endorse ideas in books made available. Although 99.7 percent of the respondents agreed that school librarians should provide a variety of points of view on current and historic issues, and 92.1 percent agreed that librarians should make even unpopular points of view available, not everyone agreed when application items became specific about the points of view. For example, while 79.99 percent favored providing conservative or liberal political literature, a lower 73.8 percent agreed when specific conservative publications were named. Almost 20 percent of the respondents selected "uncertain" in response to this item. It appears that when the application items represented especially difficult decisions or became specific about applying the principles of intellectual freedom, respondents tended to remain uncommitted, by selecting "uncertain." However, all respondents agreed that students needed a variety of resources to help develop critical thinking skills.

Table 29

Intellectual Freedom and Censorship Attitudes
Means and Frequencies
Diversity Category

	x̄	s.d.		f	%
Intellectual Freedom Items					
21. Secondary school librarians should provide books and other materials presenting a variety of points of view on current and historic issues.	4.729	.485	a* u* d*	327 0 1	99.7 0.0 0.3
35. Secondary school librarians need not endorse every idea in the books they make available.	4.540	.557	a u d	324 1 3	98.7 0.3 0.9
40. Secondary school librarians should make available the widest diversity of views and expressions, including those which are unpopular with the majority.	4.195	.639	a u d	302 20 6	92.1 6.1 1.8
Application Items					
14. School librarians should be especially watchful to see that books containing unorthodox views are kept from secondary school library collections.	4.418	.721	a u d	9 18 301	2.7 5.5 91.7
19. Secondary school librarians should not purchase conservative publications such as the *Moral Majority Newsletter* and *Conservative Digest*.	3.838	.791	a u d	22 64 242	6.7 19.5 73.8

*a agree
*u uncertain
*d disagree

Table 29 (continued)

Intellectual Freedom and Censorship Attitudes
Means and Frequencies
Diversity Category

	x̄	s.d.		f	%
25. A secondary school library is no place for either conservative or liberal extremist political literature.	3.963	.816	a u d	20 46 262	6.1 14.0 79.9
28. Secondary school students need to have access to a variety of resources to help to develop critical thinking skills.	4.659	.475	a u d	328 0 0	100.0 0.0 0.0

Access

Access items described the principle that librarians should make resources available to students without barriers such as limiting circulation, sequestering resources on restricted shelves, or labeling resources with the intent of influencing or controlling use of the resources.

School librarians agreed with the two intellectual freedom items that students should be able to choose freely from and consider a variety of points of view (96.6 percent and 99.1 percent). However, in responding to application items, school librarians were uncertain or agreed with restricting access to class use (33.7 percent), controlling circulation (17.4 percent), establishing restricted shelves (16.1 percent), or limiting interlibrary loan (15.8 percent). And 12.1 percent agreed or were uncertain about starring controversial titles to alert users.

In this category, all of the application items showed relatively large numbers of respondents selecting the "uncertain" choice rather than expressing their attitudes. The percentages of respondents selecting "uncertain" ranged from 9.1 (restricted shelves), to 13.5 percent in response to the item referring to limiting the use of resources to class use. Perhaps the items reflected practices in the respondent's school libraries, and using the "uncertain" option allowed respondents to reflect their practices but also not agree with a restrictive practice in violation of their professional principles.

Table 30

Intellectual Freedom and Censorship Attitudes
Means and Frequencies
Access Category

	x̄	s.d.		f	%
Intellectual Freedom Items					
23. Secondary school students should have the freedom to read and consider a wider range of ideas than those that may be held by the majority in the community.	4.415	.610	a* u* d*	317 6 5	96.6 1.8 1.5
34. Secondary school librarians should make it possible for students to choose freely from a variety of points of view on controversial subjects.	4.497	.530	a u d	325 2 1	99.1 0.6 0.3
Application Items					
13. Some books should be marked "for class use only" so they will be used with the guidance of a teacher.	3.694	1.084	a u d	66 44 217	20.2 13.5 66.4
17. Since secondary school librarians are in a position to recognize dangerous ideas in books and other printed materials, they should carefully control their circulation to students.	4.153	.901	a u d	24 33 270	7.3 10.1 82.6

Table 30 (continued)

Intellectual Freedom and Censorship Attitudes
Frequencies Means and
Access Category

	x̄	s.d.		f	%
26. Books about controversial subjects should be starred as a guide for students who wish to avoid works of this type.	4.171	.713	a u d	10 30 288	3.0 9.1 87.8
29. Controversial books in secondary school libraries should be kept on restricted shelves.	4.116	.852	a u d	23 30 275	7.0 9.1 83.9
38. Students should not use interlibrary loan to acquire books that the librarian has determined are not appropriate for the secondary school library collection.	4.116	.757	a u d	11 41 276	3.3 12.5 84.1

*a   agree
*u   uncertain
*d   disagree

Selection

Selection items illustrated the motivation of librarians when selecting resources, the processes used to select resources for purchase, and influences on selection decisions.

All but one respondent agreed that librarians should give meaning to freedom to read by providing resources that enrich the quality of thought and expression—an intellectual freedom item. An unexpected finding was that 43 subjects were uncertain or disagreed with the basic intellectual freedom principle that materials should not be excluded because of the background or views of the authors. Twenty-nine respondents were uncertain or disagreed with resisting efforts of groups imposing their views on the school library.

Table 31

Intellectual Freedom and Censorship Attitudes:
Means and Frequencies
Selection Category

	x̄	s.d.		f	%
Intellectual Freedom Items					
16. Secondary school librarians should not exclude materials because of the origin, background, or views of the authors.	4.146	1.024	a* u* d*	285 10 33	86.9 3.0 10.1
27. Secondary school librarians, as guardians of the students' freedom to read, should resist efforts of individuals or groups seeking to impose their views upon the school library.	4.311	.779	a u d	299 13 16	91.1 4.0 4.9
32. It is the responsibility of librarians to give full meaning to the freedom to read by providing books that enrich the quality of thought and expression.	4.521	.536	a u d	324 3 1	98.8 .9 .3
Application Items					
12. The secondary school librarian's moral and aesthetic values should be the standard for determining what books should be included in the school library collection.	4.128	.947	a u d	29 14 284	8.9 4.3 86.8
15. Secondary school librarians should avoid purchasing books that might arouse local critics.	4.110	.813	a u d	20 29 279	6.1 8.8 85.0

Table 31 (continued)

Intellectual Freedom and Censorship
Means and Frequencies
Selection Category

	x̄	s.d.		f	%
18. Secondary school librarians should avoid purchasing works of fiction dealing with social, psychological, and sexual problems and concentrate more on building collections of classics.	4.485	.553	a u d	1 6 321	.3 1.8 97.9
31. If a secondary school librarian has ordered a controversial but positively reviewed book, and now that book is the object of court action in another school in the state, the librarian should cancel the order.	4.192	.701	a u d	9 25 294	2.7 7.6 89.6
33. Secondary school librarians should not purchase books which might offend the school principal.	4.216	.699	a u d	10 19 299	3.0 5.8 91.1
37. Some issues, such as homosexuality, are just too controversial for a secondary school library.	4.335	.648	a u d	6 11 311	1.8 3.4 94.9
39. Parents should be able to expect that the books in a secondary school library will not undermine their family values.	3.333	1.001	a u d	82 78 267	25.0 23.9 51.1
41. Secondary school librarians should not select books that present our government in an unfavorable light.	3.924	.841	a u d	26 36 266	7.9 1.0 81.1

*a   agree
*u   uncertain
*d   disagree

When responding to application items illustrating the effects of outside forces on selection decisions, 14.9 percent agreed or were uncertain about the influence of local critics, 10.3 percent agreed or were uncertain about the influence of the courts, and 8.8 percent agreed or were uncertain about the principal influencing selection. But 82 respondents (25 percent) agreed that parents should expect that books in a secondary school library would not undermine family values. Only 8.9 percent agreed that the librarian's moral and aesthetic values should be the standard for selecting resources. Most librarians (94.9 percent) rejected the idea that some issues are too controversial for a secondary school library.

Similar to the other categories, the "uncertain" choice was used more than had been expected. One item, describing the influence of the expectations of parents, used a phrase commonly expressed by individuals seeking to restrict access to resources in a school library: "undermine family values." In response to this item, 78 respondents (23.9 percent) selected the "uncertain" option. Another item representing a frequently voiced concern about resources in a school library, that of presenting the government in an unfavorable light, also elicited a relatively large number of "uncertain" responses (36 or 11 percent). Indecision about the role of the courts was reflected in the 25 "uncertain" responses to whether a legal action in another district should influence the selection activities of a librarian.

Table 32

Differences in Means on Intellectual Freedom
Attitude Scale and Censorship Attitude Scale: T-Test

	x̄	s.d.	x̄ dif.	corr	t value	prob
IF mean	4.4334	.419	.3296	.694	15.90	.000
C mean	4.1039					

To explore consistency between intellectual freedom scores and censorship scores, t-tests comparing mean scores were run. Significant differences were found (t value = 15.90, p <.000). This indicated that subjects showed inconsistent attitudes when applying the principles of intellectual freedom. (Differences in means in each category arranged by demographic variables can be found in Appendix G.)

SUMMARY

Although high significant correlations were found between intellectual freedom and censorship scores, subjects were not consistent in their application of intellectual freedom principles. Inconsistencies were observed in all categories, with major differences observed in responses to items related to adhering to selection policies, selecting political literature, restrictive practices, and outside influences on selection. An unexpected finding was the relatively large number of respondents who used the "uncertain" category rather than expressing their attitude. Large numbers of "uncertain" responses were observed for items related to purchasing conservative publications, effect of a censorship controversy, and parental expectations of effects of resources on family values.Most subjects were neither strongly in agreement with intellectual freedom principles nor strongly in disagreement with restrictive practices. Almost 55 percent of the respondents fell into the middle category on both scales, with 70 percent in the middle category on the censorship scale and 64.1 percent in the middle category on the intellectual freedom scale.

REFERENCES

Busha, Charles H. "The Attitudes of Midwestern Public Librarians Toward Intellectual Freedom and Censorship." Doctoral dissertation, Indiana University, 1971.
Douma, Rollin. "Censorship in the English Classroom: A Review of

Research." *Journal of Research and Development in Education* 9 (1976), 60–68.

Farley, John J. "Book Censorship in the Senior High Libraries of Nassau County, New York." Doctoral dissertation, New York University, 1964.

Fiske, Marjorie (Lowenthal). *Book Selection and Censorship: A Study of School and Public Librarians in California.* Berkeley: University of California Press, 1959.

CHAPTER 9
INTELLECTUAL FREEDOM,
CENSORSHIP, AND MORAL REASONING

Moral reasoning was selected as a variable for this study because of the close connection between justice and rights and access to information. If one individual has access to information, all individuals must therefore have access to information. If one individual has the right to choose what to read or hear or see, then all persons have the right to determine what they will read, hear, or see. The theory of moral development and intellectual freedom principles are both based on universal principles of justice and rights for all. The "Library Bill of Rights," based on the First Amendment, affirms that all persons have the right to access any and all ideas. Moral judgments involve universal principles of justice for all individuals at all times and in all places.

Librarians reasoning at preconventional levels view censorship situations on an individual level in terms of themselves. If protecting access benefits the librarian and does not lead to adverse effects, the librarian probably would protect access rights. At conventional levels, moral judgment concerns group or social norms. At conventional levels, librarians could approach censorship from one of two stages. Stage 3 librarians would view intellectual freedom from group norms and see protecting access as part of the role of the librarian. That is, "good librarians" protect access. However, if group identification with other professionals in the school were stronger, the librarian would acquiesce to wishes of the school group to avoid trouble rather than follow the dictates of the library value system. At stage 4, the wishes of authority figures could influence how librarians view censorship situations. If the views of administrators, department chairs, and others in positions of authority seem to be restrictive, or if school rules are prohibitive, stage 4 librarians would obey rules or obey the principal. Postconventional (stage 5 and stage 6) librarians focus on justice and rights for all and would resist attempts to restrict resources based on group or social norms.

INTELLECTUAL FREEDOM, CENSORSHIP, AND MORAL REASONING

Two null hypotheses were tested:

There is no significant relationship between the principled moral reasoning of secondary school librarians as measured by the *Defining Issues Test* and their attitudes toward intellectual freedom as measured by the *Intellectual Freedom Attitude Scale.*

There is no significant relationship between the principled moral reasoning of secondary school librarians as measured by the *Defining Issues Test* and their attitudes toward censorship as measured by the *Censorship Attitude Scale.*

Both null hypotheses were rejected. Principled moral reasoning (P score) showed a significant correlation (r = .2468, p <.001) with intellectual freedom scores. Significant correlations were also found between censorship scores and P scores (r .3325, p <.001) and combined scores and P scores

Table 33

Correlations Between Intellectual Freedom and
Censorship Attitude Scores and P Scores

	P Scores
IF Scores	.2468**
C Scores	.3325**
IF/C Scores	.3298**

** p <.001

(r .3298, p <.001). These results should be viewed as statistically significant, but of little practical significance. Borg (1983: 624) pointed out that correlations this low have meaning in exploratory relationship research such as this in helping to understand complex behavior patterns, but have little value for prediction.

Rest (1986: 177) found an average P score of 40 among adult subjects. The average P score among the subjects in this study was 44 ($\bar{x}$ = 44.336). Rest also reported a well-established connection between level of education and level of moral reasoning. The results here confirmed the connection between moral reasoning and level of education. Subjects in this study were highly educated, holding master's degrees or more.

Table 34

Intellectual Freedom Attitude Scores and Principled Morality

Intellectual Freedom Score	Low (6.9–27)	P Scores Middle (28–41)	High (42–90)	Total
Low (34–40)	9 4.1%	14 6.4%	21 9.6%	44 20.1%
Middle (41–48)	17 7.8%	33 15.1%	73 33.3%	123 56.2%
High (49–50)	4 1.8%	11 5.0%	37 16.9%	52 23.7%
Totals for Each Group	30 13.7%	58 26.5%	131 59.8%	
Grand Total				219 100.0%

Intellectual Freedom Score mean = 44.526
Standard deviation = 4.179
P Score mean = 44.336
Standard deviation = 13.695

Using the divisions suggested by Rest (1979), subjects were divided into high, middle, and low groups. This arrangement of P scores revealed 131 subjects with high P scores compared with only 30 with low P scores. Nine subjects had low P scores and low Intellectual Freedom scores. Thirty-seven subjects scored high on the *Intellectual Freedom Attitude Scale* and had high P scores. Of interest were the 21 (9.6 percent) subjects with high P scores and low intellectual freedom scores. Only two subjects with high censorship scores, indicating disagreement with restrictive attitudes, had low P scores. This arrangement provided descriptive information only. Scores were not grouped for the statistical analysis.

Table 35

Censorship Attitude Scores and Principled Morality

Intellectual Freedom Score	Low (6.9–27)	P Scores Middle (28–41)	High (42–90)	Total
Low (50–73)	10 4.6%	10 4.6%	13 6.0%	33 15.2%
Middle (74–92)	18 8.3%	41 18.9%	86 39.6%	145 66.8%
High (93–100)	2 .9%	6 2.8%	31 14.3%	39 18.0%
Totals	30 13.8%	57 26.3%	130 59.9%	
Grand Total				217 100.0%

Censorship Score mean = 82.886
Standard deviation = 9.798
P Score mean = 44.336
Standard deviation = 13.695

INCOMPLETE TESTS: COMPARISON WITH COMPLETE TESTS

Because of incomplete or inconsistent responses, a large number of subjects' *DIT* scores were not available. While only 38 *Intellectual Freedom/Censorship Attitude Scale* responses were incomplete or unusable, 118 subjects, representing 32.2 percent of the sample, were rejected for incomplete results or failure to pass the consistency check on the *DIT*. Twenty-three subjects were rejected for having more than eight errors or two stories with inconsistencies in responses. Twelve subjects were rejected for checking more than eight $\underline{M}$ items, and 83 respondents had missing ranks or ratings. To determine whether there were differences between subjects who completed all portions of the survey and subjects who completed only the intellectual freedom/censorship part of the survey, t-tests were used to examine the intellectual freedom and censorship means of both groups of subjects. Differences were noted. Subjects who completed only the intellectual freedom/ censorship portion of the test exhibited lower means on the

Table 36

Subjects Who Completed Only the Intellectual
Freedom/Censorship Attitude Scale and Subjects Who Completed
the Attitude Scales and the DIT

Test	n	x̄	sd	t value	df	prob
IF and DIT	230	44.5261	4.179	1.41	326	.159
IF only	98	43.8163	4.148			
C and DIT	228	82.8860	9.798	2.22	321	.027
C only	95	80.1368	10.853			
IF/C and DIT	228	127.4211	13.060	2.10	321	.036
IF/C only	95	123.9895	14.042			

IF - *Intellectual Freedom Attitude Scale*
C - *Censorship Attitude Scale*
IF/C - *Intellectual Freedom/Censorship Attitude Scale*
DIT - *Defining Issues Test*

Intellectual Freedom Attitude Scale and the *Censorship Attitude Scale* than subjects who completed the attitude scales and the *DIT*. While the intellectual freedom scores showed no significant difference (p = .159), significant differences were observed on the censorship test (p = .027) and the combined test (p = .036).

SUMMARY

Moral reasoning provided only a modest, though significant, explanation of differences in intellectual freedom and censorship attitudes of the secondary school librarians in this study. Of importance, however, is the finding by Rest that education is the most significant variable in moral reasoning. The subjects in the study were highly educated, holding master's degrees or more. P scores reflect the level of education of these school librarians. While the results in the study might lead to a dismissal of moral development as a factor in restrictive attitudes, moral reasoning is only one of the components leading to moral behavior. Other developmental characteristics, including ego strength, might provide further explanation of differences between individuals in applying the principles of the profession.

REFERENCES

Borg, Walter R., and Meredith Damien Gall. *Educational Research: An Introduction.* 4th ed. New York: Longman, 1983.

Rest, James R. *Moral Development: Advances in Research and Theory.* New York: Praeger, 1986.

CHAPTER 10
DISCUSSION OF FINDINGS

The results of this exploratory study of the attitudes of secondary school librarians in Iowa, Minnesota, and Wisconsin showed that level of education of school librarians, preparation programs, and size of school were significantly related to attitudes toward intellectual freedom. Level of education of the school librarian, size of school, and grade levels in school were significantly related to attitudes toward censorship. Other variables (age, location of school district, and years of experience) showed no significant relationships to attitudes toward intellectual freedom or censorship. Principled moral reasoning showed a significant, though modest, relationship to intellectual freedom attitudes and censorship attitudes.

The first research question asked whether there was a significant relationship between attitudes toward intellectual freedom and attitudes toward censorship. As expected, significant relationships were observed ($r = .6937$, $p < .001$). Subjects who agreed with intellectual freedom principles tended to agree with the application of the principles. However, inconsistencies were observed (Intellectual Freedom and Censorship mean differences t value 15.90, $p < .000$). Subjects agreed more with intellectual freedom principles than with application of the principles. Inconsistent attitudes were observed in all categories of practices.

Although expected, the inconsistencies between attitudes toward intellectual freedom and attitudes toward censorship illustrate that knowing the principles of the profession is no guarantee that those principles will be applied in actual practice. While an exploratory correlation study does not predict behavior, if the attitudes reported in this study were translated into behavior, the school librarians would not be acting to provide unrestricted access to information. The application items developed for this study represented real situations, and the number of respondents who apparently did not transfer intellectual freedom principles to practical situations indicates that speculation about self-censorship is probably accurate. Whether the inconsistencies observed reflect actual practice in school libraries, represent school librarians unable to translate theory to practice, or illustrate a lack of understanding of how professional principles are applied in real situations, the responses of the school librarians in this study did not reflect the values of their profession.

INTELLECTUAL FREEDOM ATTITUDES

The hypothesis that demographic characteristics of school librarians would be related to attitudes toward intellectual freedom was rejected in part. Level of education and size of school were found to be significantly related to intellectual freedom attitudes. Librarians with master's degrees held more positive attitudes toward intellectual freedom than librarians with bachelor's degrees, confirming findings in previous studies that level of education influences attitudes toward intellectual freedom. Librarians in schools with more than 1,000 students showed more agreement with intellectual freedom items than librarians in schools with fewer than 500 students. No significant differences were found between attitudes toward intellectual freedom and geographical location of subjects. While the gender of respondents was not significant in this study, in 1971 Busha found that male public librarians were more likely to agree with intellectual freedom principles than female public librarians. Age and years of experience were not significantly related to attitudes toward intellectual freedom.

CENSORSHIP ATTITUDES

Level of education, size of school, and grade levels in school were significantly related to censorship attitudes. As size of school increased, restrictive attitudes decreased. Librarians with master's degrees were less restrictive than librarians with bachelor's degrees. Busha (1971), England (1974), and Pope (1974) found that female librarians were more restrictive than male librarians, but gender was not found to be significant in this study. Although Busha found a significant relationship between attitudes and younger librarians and a steady, though not significant, increase in restrictive attitudes as age increased, significant relationships based on age were not found in this study. However, the youngest and oldest groups showed lower mean scores than librarians in the middle age groups.

EDUCATION AND ATTITUDES

Level of education appears to be emerging as a significant variable in studies of attitudes toward intellectual freedom and censorship. For state licensing agencies, the message is clear. If access to information is of concern, the master's degree should be required for licensure or certification. In the last analysis of certification requirements reported by Perritt (1988), the master's degree was found to be required for entry-level school library media specialist certification in only two states—Alabama and North Carolina—and in the District of Columbia. Two other states list the master's degree as one of two options for certification. Twelve states require master's degrees for second or advanced levels of certification. Of the three population states, Iowa and Wisconsin require 24 credit hours and Minnesota requires 36 credit hours of library media course work for entry-level school library media certification. All three states require master's degrees for advanced-level school library media certification. Although *Information Power* endorsed the master's degree as the entry-level degree for the profession, it is perhaps too early for states to have revised their licensing/certification requirements to reflect recommendations of national guidelines for school library media professionals. Therefore, the influence of *Information Power* on state certification requirements has not yet been recorded.

PROFESSIONAL MEMBERSHIPS AND ATTITUDES

It was hypothesized that membership in a professional organization would not be related to attitudes toward intellectual freedom and censorship. Significant differences were found between members of professional organizations and nonmembers. Members of the American Library Association and the American Association of School Librarians showed higher mean scores on the Intellectual Freedom Attitude Scale than nonmembers. In contrast, membership in the Association for Educational Communications and Technology was not found to be significant. State membership was significant overall, but memberships in specific state organizations, while revealing higher mean scores among members, did not reveal significant differences, except for Iowa respondents. Subjects from Iowa who were members of the Iowa Educational Media Association had significantly higher scores on the *Intellectual Freedom Attitude Scale* than subjects from Iowa who were not members of the state organization. Members of state and national organizations showed higher means on the *Censorship Attitude Scale* than nonmembers, but a level of significance was reached only by Iowa respondents.

MORAL REASONING AND ATTITUDES

It was hypothesized that there would be a relationship between level of moral reasoning and attitudes toward intellectual freedom and censorship. Significant correlations were found, although the relationships were modest (Intellectual Freedom $r = .2468$, $p < .001$, and Censorship $r = .3324$, $p < .001$). Although both relationships were small, the size of the relationship between principled moral reasoning and the application items, or censorship, was larger than the relationship between principled moral reasoning and intellectual freedom items. Perhaps agreeing with the intellectual freedom items representing principles held by the profession of librarianship entailed less reasoning than applying the principles. Or, perhaps, applying the principles required moral reasoning, but agreeing with intellectual freedom principles represented rote responses.

UNHYPOTHESIZED FINDING

An unexpected finding was the relationship between institution of educational preparation and attitudes toward intellectual freedom and censorship. In a comparison of all subjects, those who had attended library education programs accredited by the American Library Association had significantly higher mean scores on the *Intellectual Freedom Attitude Scale* than subjects from other library education programs (Intellectual Freedom t value 3.08, p =.002). Additional analysis comparing only subjects with master's degrees affirmed the finding, though at a lower level of significance. Subjects with master's degrees from ALA programs scored significantly higher on the *Intellectual Freedom Attitude Scale* (t value 1.96, p = .052) than subjects with master's degrees from other preparation programs. Perhaps persons inclined to agree with intellectual freedom principles selected the accredited programs, or perhaps the environment in a program accredited by the American Library Association is more conducive to accepting professional principles, or perhaps accredited schools place more emphasis on the ethics of the profession than other schools. Another explanation could be that subjects from ALA programs take some, perhaps most, of their course work with persons preparing to work as librarians in public and academic libraries, environments in which intellectual freedom is expected and this expectation is carried into the school. Education courses in state and private colleges and universities, on the other hand, are usually attended by individuals who are working in schools where the professional ethic does not include intellectual freedom concepts. Further, school librarians work in an atmosphere in which protection of children appears to be the norm and work with professional colleagues who have not had educational preparation in the principles of intellectual freedom.

When comparing subjects at all educational levels on the *Censorship Attitude Scale,* significant differences between subjects from ALA programs and subjects from other programs were found. However, the level of significance was much less than the level reached for intellectual freedom attitude scores (Censorship t value 2.16, p =.032). When level of education was the variable, additional analysis showed no significant differences between subjects with master's degrees from ALA programs and subjects with master's degrees from other programs on the *Censorship Attitude Scale* (t value 1.00, p = .317). Application of the principles of intellectual freedom or attitudes toward restrictive practices is no different among ALA graduates than among graduates from other programs. Level of education is a more significant variable in explaining differences in attitudes toward censorship than institution of educational preparation.

SUMMARY OF FINDINGS

In this study, the variables most significantly related to intellectual freedom attitudes were size of school, level of education, memberships in professional organizations, and institution of educational preparation. Size of school, grade levels in school, level of education, and professional memberships were found to be significantly related to attitudes toward censorship. Principled morality was only slightly related to intellectual freedom and censorship attitudes.

Decisions about selecting resources and making resources available are extremely complex. The exploratory and descriptive findings reported here, while generally supporting previous research related to certain demographic variables, suggested that moral reasoning as a personal variable provided only a modest explanation of differences among school librarians in attitudes toward intellectual freedom and censorship. However, moral reasoning is only one of the personal characteristics that might have an effect on attitudes. Busha (1971) found much higher relationships between authoritarian beliefs and intellectual freedom and censorship attitudes in the public librarians who he investigated than were found in this study of another personal characteristic: level of principled moral reasoning among school librarians.

IMPLICATIONS FOR FUTURE RESEARCH

Other than Busha's (1971) investigation of the authoritarian beliefs of public librarians, no other researcher has examined such personal characteristics as level of moral reasoning, authoritarian beliefs, or ego strength of librarians. This study represented a first step in the process of isolating personal and developmental variables related to intellectual freedom and censorship attitudes among school librarians. Much additional research must be conducted before personal characteristic profiles of school librarians and attitudes toward censorship and intellectual freedom can be constructed.

Since the Fiske (1959) and Busha (1971) studies of attitudes of librarians toward intellectual freedom and censorship, it has been known that not all librarians translate professional beliefs into practice. To understand the reasons, researchers need to gather data from a variety of measures and, using more sophisticated research techniques (such as factor analysis and multiple regression), isolate the variables that contribute significantly to attitudes toward intellectual freedom and censorship.

As Serebnick (1979) pointed out, librarian variables are only one of many variables influencing selection and censorship in libraries. In addition to librarian variables, Serebnick identified library, community, mass media, and judicial and legal factors as variables affecting selection and censorship in libraries. Serebnick's list referred to public libraries, but the variables listed could be adapted for schools as well. Research is needed on all variables. For example, Fiske (1959) found the attitudes of principals to be a significant determining factor in the restrictiveness of school librarians. Responses in this study also illustrated the influence of school administrators on selection and removal of resources. Two items referred to school principals. In both instances, respondents showed inconsistencies between responses to intellectual freedom items and application items measuring the same concept. Research is needed on the attitudes of the individuals with whom the school librarian works and how those attitudes influence the behavior of school librarians.

Attitudes represent only one step in the value system leading to moral behavior. Rest (1986) defined a four-component model representing the "process involved in the production of a moral act." Efforts must be made to translate censorship situations to Rest's four-component model of behavior in a moral situation.

The finding in this study that school librarians from ALA accredited programs showed significantly higher scores on the *Intellectual Freedom Attitude Scale* needs further study. Because most school librarians throughout the country receive their professional preparation in institutions of higher education where the library education program is not accredited by the American Library Association, efforts must be made to make sure that preparation programs in higher education institutions accredited by NCATE and other state and regional accrediting agencies provide the same attention to the principles of the profession as do programs accredited by the American Library Association. Further study is needed before conclusions about differences in preparation programs that might account for significantly different attitudes toward intellectual freedom can be reached with some confidence. Certainly if the trends observed here represent results that are replicated in future studies, faculty from colleges of education accredited by NCATE and other institutions of higher education preparing school librarians need to examine what is taught about intellectual freedom concepts. Research on curriculum and teaching and learning strategies might suggest reasons for differences. Faculty from programs not accredited by the American Library Association need to examine the environment, the curriculum, their attitudes, and the attitudes of colleagues to determine why differences in intellectual freedom attitudes were found between their graduates and those from library schools whose programs are accredited by the American Library Association.

Based on the findings in this study, all programs need to pay more attention to the application of the principles of intellectual freedom. Apparently students learn the principles of the profession but fail to learn how to apply the principles. If the preparation programs emphasize low levels of cognitive learning, and fail to focus on application and synthesis of learning, students will not be able to translate knowing to applying.

Research is needed on the intellectual freedom and censorship attitudes of faculty. Perhaps faculty in programs accredited by the American Library Association hold different attitudes toward intellectual freedom and censorship than faculty in other schools. Educational preparation was found to be a significant factor among the school librarians in this study. Research is also needed to determine whether the educational preparation of faculty contributes to their attitudes toward intellectual freedom and censorship. If educational preparation influences attitudes, perhaps educational preparation of faculty also influences how concepts of intellectual freedom and censorship are taught.

Finally, attitudes do not predict behavior in a censorship situation. Case study research on incidents of censorship must be conducted and examined to determine variables related to actual behavior in censorship incidents.

IMPLICATIONS OF THE STUDY

This study revealed that school librarians, while professing agreement with the principles of intellectual freedom, were not so strongly in agreement with application of the principles. School librarians were inclined to be restrictive in all categories of potential censorship: policy, selection, access, and diversity. School librarians showed restrictive attitudes toward selection of resources, responded to perceived influences on their selection decisions, seemed unwilling to enforce policies protecting resources, and reluctant to provide unrestricted access to items in the collection.

If school librarians see themselves as part of the profession of librarianship and profess adherence to its basic principle of unrestricted access to resources for all, then application of the principles of intellectual freedom stated in professional documents must become part of their professional ethic.

Information Power (1988), national guidelines for school library programs, states that the mission of the school library media program is to ensure that students and staff are effective users of ideas and information. The mission requires that school librarians provide unrestricted physical and intellectual access to information for all library users. The results of this study indicated that if the attitudes of the school librarians were translated into behavior, school librarians would not accomplish the mission.

The implications of this study go beyond the preparation of school librarians. If the purpose of education is to prepare individuals to participate as contributing members of a pluralistic democratic society, then intellectual freedom and censorship are issues of concern to all educators. Teachers and students need access to resources to teach and learn skills of critical thinking and respect for, and understanding of, cultural diversity. Such teaching and learning occur only in an atmosphere of intellectual freedom and constitutional protections. It appears that if colleges of education are not preparing school librarians to uphold principles of access to information, they are probably not preparing teachers and administrators to value the importance of access to information either. Educators holding restrictive attitudes contribute to a restrictive atmosphere in which freedom to teach and access to information are compromised. Preparation for living in a democratic society requires an education in which the principles of freedom to read are modeled and an intellectual freedom environment is the norm, rather than the exception.

Finally, while the results reported here showed some differences among the subjects in this sample, conclusions may not be applied to all school librarians in the population states, nor to school librarians in other areas of the country. However, the verification of findings from previous research suggests that certain variables, such as level of educational preparation, may be related to attitudes toward intellectual freedom and censorship.

REFERENCES

American Association of School Librarians. *Information Power: Guidelines for School Library Media Programs.* Chicago: American Association of School Librarians and Association for Educational Communications and Technology, 1988.

Busha, Charles H. "The Attitudes of Midwestern Public Librarians Toward Intellectual Freedom and Censorship." Doctoral dissertation, Indiana University, 1971.

England, Claire St. Clere. "The Climate of Censorship in Ontario." Doctoral dissertation, University of Toronto, 1974.

Fiske, Marjorie (Lowenthal). *Book Selection and Censorship: A Study of School and Public Librarians in California.* Berkeley: University of California Press, 1959.

Perritt, Patsy H. "School Library Media Certificate Requirements: 1988 Update—Part I. *School Library Journal* 34 (June-July, 1988) 31–38.

Pope, Michael. *Sex and the Undecided Librarian: A Study of Librarians' Opinions on Sexually Oriented Literature.* Metuchen, New Jersey: Scarecrow Press, 1974.

Rest, James R. *Moral Development: Advances in Research and Theory.* New York: Praeger, 1986.

Serebnick, Judith. "An Analysis of the Relationship Between Book Reviews and the Inclusion of Potentially Controversial Books in Public Libraries." *Collection Building* 1 (1979), 8–53.

APPENDIX A

INTELLECTUAL FREEDOM DOCUMENTS

Library Bill of Rights

The American Library Association affirms that all libraries are forums for information and ideas, and that the following basic policies should guide their services.

1. Books and other library resources should be provided for the interest, information, and enlightenment of all people of the community the library serves. Materials should not be excluded because of the origin, background, or views of those contributing to their creation.

2. Libraries should provide materials and information presenting all points of view on current and historical issues. Materials should not be proscribed or removed because of partisan or doctrinal disapproval.

3. Libraries should challenge censorship in the fulfillment of their responsibility to provide information and enlightenment.

4. Libraries should cooperate with all persons and groups concerned with resisting abridgement of free expression and free access to ideas.

5. A person's right to use a library should not be denied or abridged because of origin, age, background, or views.

6. Libraries which make exhibit spaces and meeting rooms available to the public they serve should make such facilities available on an equitable basis, regardless of the beliefs or affiliations of individuals or groups requesting their use.

Adopted June 18, 1948.
Amended February 2, 1969, June 27, 1967,
and January 23, 1980,
by the ALA Council.

Access to Resources and Services in the School Library Media Program
An Interpretation of the Library Bill of Rights

The school library media program plays a unique role in promoting intellectual freedom. It serves as a point of voluntary access to information and ideas and as a learning laboratory for students as they acquire critical thinking and problem solving skills needed in a pluralistic society. Although the educational level and program of the school necessarily shape the resources and services of a school library media program, the principles of the Library Bill of Rights apply equally to all libraries, including school library media programs.

School library media professionals assume a leadership role in promoting the principles of intellectual freedom within the school by providing resources and services that create and sustain an atmosphere of free inquiry. School library media professionals work closely with teachers to integrate instructional activities in classroom units designed to equip students to locate, evaluate, and use a broad range of ideas effectively. Through resources, programming, and educational processes, students and teachers experience the free and robust debate characteristic of a democratic society.

School library media professionals cooperate with other individuals in building collections of resources appropriate to the developmental and maturity levels of students. These collections provide resources which support the curriculum and are consistent with the philosophy, goals, and objectives of the school district. Resources in school library media collections represent diverse points of view and current as well as historic issues.

While English is, by history and tradition, the customary language of the United States, the languages in use in any given community may vary. Schools serving communities in which other languages are used make efforts to accommodate the needs of students for whom English is a second language. To support these efforts, and to ensure equal access to resources and services, the school library media program provides resources which reflect the linguistic pluralism of the community.

Members of the school community involved in the collection development process employ educational criteria to select resources unfettered by their personal, political, social, or religious views. Students and educators served by the school library media program have access to resources and services free of constraints resulting from personal, partisan, or doctrinal disapproval. School library media professionals resist efforts by individuals to define what is appropriate for all students or teachers to read, view, or hear.

Major barriers between students and resources include: imposing age or grade level restrictions on the use of resources, limiting the use of interlibrary loan and access to electronic information, charging fees for information in specific formats, requiring permissions from parents or teachers, establishing restricted shelves or closed collections, and labeling. Policies, procedures, and rules related to the use of resources and services support free and open access to information.

The school board adopts policies that guarantee students access to a broad range of ideas. These include policies on collection development and procedures for the review of resources about which concerns have been raised. Such policies, developed by persons in the school community, provide for a timely and fair hearing and assure that procedures are applied equitably to all expressions of concern. School library media professionals implement district policies and procedures in the school.

Adopted July 2, 1986, by the ALA Council

On Professional Ethics, 1981

Since 1939, the American Library Association has recognized the importance of codifying and making known to the public and the profession the principles which guide librarians in action. This latest revision of the "Code of Ethics" reflects changes in the nature of the profession and in its social and institutional environment. It should be revised and augmented as necessary.

Librarians significantly influence or control the selection, organization, preservation, and dissemination of information. In a political system grounded in an informed citizenry, librarians are members of a profession explicitly committed to intellectual freedom and the freedom of access to information. We have a special obligation to ensure the free flow of information and ideas to present and future generations.

Librarians are dependent upon one another for the bibliographical resources that enable us to provide information services, and have obligations for maintaining the highest level of personal integrity and competence.

Code of Ethics

I. Librarians must provide the highest level of service through appropriate and usefully organized collections, fair and equitable circulation and service policies, and skillful, accurate, unbiased, and courteous responses to all requests for assistance.

II. Librarians must resist all efforts by groups and individuals to censor library materials.

III. Librarians must protect each user's right to privacy with respect to information sought or received, and materials consulted, borrowed, or acquired.

IV. Librarians must adhere to the principles of due process and equality of opportunity in peer relationships and personnel actions.

V. Librarians must distinguish clearly in their actions and statements between their personal philosophies and attitudes and those of an institution or professional body.

VI. Librarians must avoid situations in which personal interests might be served or financial benefits gained at the expense of library users, colleagues, or the employing institution.

American Library Association Policy 54.16 Adopted June 30, 1981, by ALA Membership and ALA Council

This Code of Ethics was current at the time of publication. The American Library Association is currently examining the document for possible revision.

Freedom To Read Statement

The freedom to read is essential to our democracy. It is continuously under attack. Private groups and public authorities in various parts of the country are working to remove books from sale, to censor textbooks, to label "controversial" books, to distribute lists of "objectionable" books or authors, and to purge libraries. These actions apparently rise from a view that our national tradition of free expression is no longer valid; that censorship and suppression are needed to avoid the subversion of politics and the corruption of morals. We, as citizens devoted to the use of books and as librarians and publishers responsible for disseminating them, wish to assert the public interest in the preservation of the freedom to read.

We are deeply concerned about these attempts at suppression. Most such attempts rest on a denial of the fundamental premise of democracy: that the ordinary citizen, by exercising critical judgment, will accept the good and reject the bad. The censors, public and private, assume that they should determine what is good and what is bad for their fellow-citizens.

We trust Americans to recognize propaganda, and to reject it. We do not believe they need the help of censors to assist them in this task. We do not believe they are prepared to sacrifice their heritage of a free press in order to be "protected" against what others think may be bad for them. We believe they still favor free enterprise in ideas and expression.

We are aware, of course, that books are not alone in being subjected to efforts at suppression. We are aware that these efforts are related to a larger pattern of pressures being brought against education, the press, films, radio, and television. The problem is not only one of actual censorship. The shadow of fear cast by these pressures leads, we suspect, to an even larger voluntary curtailment of expression by those who seek to avoid controversy.

Such pressure toward conformity is perhaps natural to a time of uneasy change and pervading fear. Especially when so many of our apprehensions are directed against an ideology, the expression of a dissident idea becomes a thing feared in itself, and we tend to move against it as against a hostile deed, with suppression.

And yet suppression is never more dangerous than in such a time of social tension. Freedom has given the United States the elasticity to endure strain. Freedom keeps open the path of novel and creative solutions, and enables change to come by choice. Every silencing of a heresy, every enforcement of an orthodoxy, diminishes the toughness and resilience of our society and leaves it the less able to deal with stress.

Now as always in our history, books are among our greatest instruments of freedom. They are almost the only means for making generally available ideas or manners of expression that can initially command only a small audience. They are the natural medium for the new ideas and the untried voice from which come the original contributions to social growth. They are essential to the extended discussion which serious thought requires, and to the accumulation of knowledge and ideas into organized collections.

We believe that free communication is essential to the preservation of a free society and a creative culture. We believe that these pressures towards conformity present the danger of limiting the range and variety of inquiry and expression on which our democracy and our culture depend. We believe that every American community must jealously guard the freedom to publish and to circulate, in order to preserve its own freedom to read. We believe that publishers and librarians have a profound responsibility to give validity to that freedom to read by making it possible for the readers to choose freely from a variety of offerings.

The freedom to read is guaranteed by the Constitution. Those with faith in free people will stand firm on these

constitutional guarantees of essential rights and will exercise
the responsibilities that accompany these rights.

We therefore affirm these propositions:

1. *It is in the public interest for publishers and librarians to make available the widest diversity of views and expressions, including those which are unorthodox or unpopular with the majority.*

Creative thought is by definition new, and what is new
is different. The bearer of every new thought is a rebel
until that idea is refined and tested. Totalitarian systems attempt to maintain themselves in power by the
ruthless suppression of any concept which challenges
the established orthodoxy. The power of a democratic
system to adapt to change is vastly strengthened by the
freedom of its citizens to choose widely from among
conflicting opinions offered freely to them. To stifle
every nonconformist idea at birth would mark the end
of the democratic process. Furthermore, only through
the constant activity of weighing and selecting can the
democratic mind attain the strength demanded by
times like these. We need to know not only what we
believe but why we believe it.

2. *Publishers, librarians, and booksellers do not need to endorse every idea or presentation contained in the books they make available. It would conflict with the public interest for them to establish their own political, moral, or aesthetic views as a standard for determining what books should be published or circulated.*

Publishers and librarians serve the educational process by helping to make available knowledge and
ideas required for the growth of the mind and the
increase of learning. They do not foster education by
imposing as mentors the patterns of their own
thought. The people should have the freedom to read
and consider a broader range of ideas than those that

may be held by any single librarian or publisher or government or church. It is wrong that what one can read should be confined to what another thinks proper.

3. *It is contrary to the public interest for publishers or librarians to determine the acceptability of a book on the basis of the personal history or political affiliations of the author.*

A book should be judged as a book. No art or literature can flourish if it is to be measured by the political views or private lives of its creators. No society of free people can flourish which draws up lists of writers to whom it will not listen, whatever they may have to say.

4. *There is no place in our society for efforts to coerce the taste of others, to confine adults to the reading matter deemed suitable for adolescents, or to inhibit the efforts of writers to achieve artistic expression.*

To some, much of modern literature is shocking. But is not much of life itself shocking? We cut off literature at the source if we prevent writers from dealing with the stuff of life. Parents and teachers have a responsibility to prepare the young to meet the diversity of experiences in life to which they will be exposed, as they have a responsibility to help them learn to think critically for themselves. These are affirmative responsibilities, not be be discharged simply by preventing them from reading works for which they are not yet prepared. In these matters taste differs, and taste cannot be legislated; nor can machinery be devised which will suit the demands of one group without limiting the freedom of others.

5. *It is not in the public interest to force a reader to accept with any book the prejudgment of a label characterizing the book or author as subversive or dangerous.*

The idea of labeling presupposes the existence of individuals or groups with wisdom to determine by authority what is good or bad for the citizen. It presupposes that individuals must be directed in making up their minds about the ideas they examine. But Americans do not need others to do their thinking for them.

6. *It is the responsibility of publishers and librarians, as guardians of the people's freedom to read, to contest encroachments upon that freedom by individuals or groups seeking to impose their own standards or tastes upon the community at large.*

It is inevitable in the give and take of the democratic process that the political, the moral, or the aesthetic concepts of an individual or group will occasionally collide with those of another individual or group. In a free society individuals are free to determine for themselves what they wish to read, and each group is free to determine what it will recommend to its freely associated members. But no group has the right to take the law into its own hands, and to impose its own concept of politics or morality upon other members of a democratic society. Freedom is no freedom if it is accorded only to the accepted and the inoffensive.

7. *It is the responsibility of publishers and librarians to give full meaning to the freedom to read by providing books that enrich the quality and diversity of thought and expression. By the exercise of this affirmative responsibility, they can demonstrate that the answer to a bad book is a good one, the answer to a bad idea is a good one.*

The freedom to read is of little consequence when expended on the trivial; it is frustrated when the reader cannot obtain matter fit for that reader's purpose. What is needed is not only the absence of restraint, but the positive provision of opportunity for

the people to read the best that has been thought and
said. Books are the major channel by which the
intellectual inheritance is handed down, and the
principal means of its testing and growth. The defense
of their freedom and integrity, and the enlargement
of their service to society, requires of all publishers
and librarians the utmost of their faculties, and
deserves of all citizens the fullest of their support.

We state these propositions neither lightly nor as easy
generalizations. We here stake out a lofty claim for the value
of books. We do so because we believe that they are good,
possessed of enormous variety and usefulness, worthy of
cherishing and keeping free. We realize that the application of
these propositions may mean the dissemination of ideas and
manners of expression that are repugnant to many persons.
We do not state these propositions in the comfortable belief
that what people read is unimportant. We believe rather that
what people read is deeply important; that ideas can be
dangerous; but that the suppression of ideas is fatal to a
democratic society. Freedom itself is a dangerous way of life,
but it is ours.

---

*This statement was originally issued in May 1953 by the
Westchester Conference of the American Library Association and
the American Book Publishers Council, which in 1970 consolidated with the American Educational Publishers Institute to
become the Association of American Publishers. Adopted June 25,
1953. Revised January 28, 1972, January 16, 1991, by the ALA
Council and the AAP Freedom to Read Committee.*

APPENDIX B

KOHLBERG THEORY OF MORAL DEVELOPMENT*

* "The Six Stages of Moral Development" from *The Philosophy of Moral Development*, by Lawrence Kohlberg. Copyright © 1981 by Lawrence Kohlberg. Reprinted by permission of Harper Collins Publishers.

Level A. Preconventional Level

Stage 1. The Stage of Punishment and Obedience
Content

Right is literal obedience to rules and authority, avoiding punishment, and not doing physical harm.

1. What is right is to avoid breaking rules, to obey for obedience's sake, and to avoid doing physical damage to people and property.
2. The reasons for doing right are avoidance of punishment and the superior power of authorities.

Social Perspective

This stage takes an egocentric point of view. A person at this stage doesn't consider the interests of others or recognize they differ from actor's, and doesn't relate two points of view. Actions are judged in terms of physical consequences rather than in terms of psychological interests of others. Authority's perspective is confused with one's own.

Stage 2. The Stage of Individual Instrumental Purpose and Exchange
Content

Right is serving one's own or other's needs and making fair deals in terms of concrete exchange.

1. What is right is following rules when it is to someone's immediate interest. Right is acting to meet one's own interests and needs and letting others do the same. Right is also what is fair; that is, what is an equal exchange, a deal, an agreement.
2. The reason for doing right is to serve one's own needs or interests in a world where one must

recognize that other people have their interests, too.

Social Perspective

This stage takes a concrete individualistic perspective. A person at this stage separates own interests and points of view from those of authorities and others. He or she is aware everybody has individual interests to pursue and these conflict, so that right is relative (in the concrete individualistic sense). The person integrates or relates conflicting individual interests to one another through instrumental exchange of services, through instrumental need for the other and the other's goodwill, or through fairness, giving each person the same amount.

Level B. Conventional Level

Stage 3. The Stage of Mutual Interpersonal Expectations, Relationships, and Conformity
Content

The right is playing a good (nice) role, being concerned about the other people and their feelings, keeping loyalty and trust with partners, and being motivated to follow rules and expectations.

1. What is right is living up to what is expected by people close to one or what people generally expect of people in one's role as son, sister, friend, and so on. "Being good" is important and means having good motives, showing concern about others. It also means keeping mutual relationships, maintaining trust, loyalty, respect, and gratitude.
2. Reasons for doing right are needing to be good in one's own eyes and those of others, caring for others, and because if one puts oneself in the other person's place one would want good behavior from the self (Golden Rule).

Social Perspective
> This stage takes the perspective of the individual in relationship to other individuals. A person at this stage is aware of shared feelings, agreements, and expectations, which take primacy over individual interests. The person relates points of view through the "concrete Golden Rule," putting oneself in the other person's shoes. He or she does not consider generalized "system" perspective.

Stage 4. The Stage of Social System and Conscience Maintenance
Content
> The right is doing one's duty in society, upholding the social order, and maintaining the welfare of society or the group.

> 1. What is right is fulfilling the actual duties to which one has agreed. Laws are to be upheld except in extreme cases where they conflict with other fixed social duties and rights. Right is also contributing to society, the group, or institution.
> 2. The reasons for doing right are to keep the institution going as a whole, self-respect or conscience as meeting one's defined obligations, or the consequences: "What if everyone did it?"

Social Perspective
> This stage differentiates societal point of view from interpersonal agreement or motives. A person at this stage takes the viewpoint of the system, which defines roles and rules. He or she considers individual relations in terms of place in the system.

Level B/C. Transitional Level

This level is postconventional but not yet principled.
Content of Transition
> At Stage 4 1/2, choice is personal and subjective. It is based on emotions; conscience is seen as arbitrary and

relative, as are ideas such as "duty" and "morally right."

Transitional Social Perspective
At this stage, the perspective is that of an individual standing outside of his own society and considering himself as an individual making decisions without a generalized commitment or contract with society. One can pick and choose obligations, which are defined by particular societies, but one has no principles for such choice.

Level C. Postconventional and Principled Level

Moral decisions are generated from rights, values, or principles that are (or could be) agreeable to all individuals composing or creating a society designed to have fair and beneficial practices.

Stage 5. The Stage of Prior Rights and Social Contract or Utility
Content
The right is upholding the basic rights, values, and legal contracts of a society, even when they conflict with the concrete rules and laws of the group.

1. What is right is being aware of the fact that people hold a variety of values and opinions, that most values and rules are relative to one's group. These "relative" rules should usually be upheld, however, in the interest of impartiality and because they are the social contract. Some nonrelative values and rights, such as life and liberty, however, must be upheld in any society and regardless of majority opinion.
2. Reasons for doing right are, in general, feeling obligated to obey the law because one has made a social contract to make and abide by laws for the good of all and to protect their own rights and the rights of others. Family, friendship, trust, and work

obligations are also commitments or contracts freely entered into and entail respect for the rights of others. One is concerned that laws and duties be based on rational calculation of overall utility: "the greatest good for the greatest number."

Social Perspective

This stage takes a prior-to-society perspective—that of a rational individual aware of values and rights prior to social attachments and contracts. The person integrates perspectives by formal mechanisms of agreement, contract, objective impartiality, and due process. He or she considers the moral point of view and the legal point of view, recognizes they conflict, and finds it difficult to integrate them.

Stage 6. The Stage of Universal Ethical Principles
Content

This stage assumes guidance by universal ethical principles that all humanity should follow.

1. Regarding what is right, Stage 6 is guided by universal ethical principles. Particular laws or social agreements are usually valid because they rest on such principles. When laws violate these principles, one acts in accordance with the principle. Principles are universal principles of justice: the equality of human rights and respect for the dignity of human beings as individuals. These are not merely values that are recognized, but are also principles used to generate particular decisions.

2. The reason for doing right is that, as a rational person, one has seen the validity of principles and has become committed to them.

Social Perspective

This stage takes the perspective of a moral point of view from which social arrangements derive or on which they are grounded. The perspective is that of any rational individual recognizing the nature of morality or the basic moral premise of respect for other persons as ends, not means.

Source: Lawrence Kohlberg. *The Philosophy of Moral Development: Moral Stages and the Idea of Justice.* Vol. 1 of *Essays on Moral Development.* Cambridge: Harper and Row, 1981. 409–412.

APPENDIX C

SURVEY INSTRUMENT

School Library Issues and Social Problems

An Opinion Survey

This survey attempts to identify what school librarians/media specialists think about some current library issues and some general social problems. You have probably thought about and discussed many of these issues. Different people have different opinions about these issues. Your frank opinion about each is the best answer. Whatever you think, you may be sure that some other librarians will agree with you, and some will disagree. Since your personal opinions are needed, please do not consult with others as you complete the survey.

There are three parts to this survey.

Section I asks some general information so that your opinions may be included with those of other librarians similar to you.

Section II presents some commonly held opinions about school libraries. You are being asked whether you agree or disagree with the statements.

Section III is in the form of stories about general social problems. You are being asked what you think about these problem stories.

Specific directions are included with each section of the survey.

Your opinions about these issues are of considerable value to me. I look forward to receiving your completed survey.

SECTION I.

No. _____

Please check the appropriate responses.

1. Size of school: How many students are enrolled in your school?
   _____ a. 199 and under _____ d. 500 - 999
   _____ b. 200 - 299 _____ e. 1,000 - 1,999
   _____ c. 300 - 499 _____ f. 2,000 and over

2. Grade levels in your school: (Check all that apply)
   _____ 7 _____ 8 _____ 9 _____ 10 _____ 11 _____ 12 _____ Other

3. Including this year, how many years have you worked as a school library/media professional?
   _____ a. 0–5 _____ d. 16–25
   _____ b. 6–10 _____ e. 26 and over
   _____ c. 11–15

4. Age:
   _____ a. 20–29
   _____ b. 30–39
   _____ c. 40–49
   _____ d. 50–59
   _____ e. 60 and over

5. Sex:
   _____ a. male
   _____ b. female

6. Level of education: (Check your most advanced degree)
   _____ a. B.A. or B.S. degree
   _____ b. B.A. or B.S. degree plus additional undergraduate or graduate credits
   _____ c. M.A. or M.S. or M.Ed degree
   _____ d. M.A. or M.S. or M.Ed degree plus additional graduate credits
   _____ e. Specialist degree
   _____ f. Ed.D. or Ph.D.

7. Library/media courses for your license or certificate taken at:
   _____ a. Private college or university
   _____ b. State college or university
   _____ c. ALA accredited library school

8. Are you a member of your state professional library/media organization?
   _____ a. Yes _____ b. No (If no, go to question 10)

9. Check all that apply:
    Iowa: _____ a. IEMA   Wisconsin: _____ e. WEMA
                    _____ b. ILA   _____ f. WLA
    Minnesota: _____ c. MEMO
                    _____ d. MLA

10. Are you a member of your national professional library/media organization?
    _____ a. Yes   _____b. No (If no, skip question 11)

11. Check all that apply:
    _____ a. ALA _____b. AASL _____c. AECT _____d. DSMS

SECTION II. SCHOOL LIBRARY ISSUES

Please indicate your opinion of the following statements by circling the appropriate response.

SA	Strongly Agree
A	Agree
U	Uncertain
D	Disagree
SD	Strongly Disagree

12. The secondary school librarian's moral and aesthetic values should be the standard for determining what books should be included in the school library collection.   SA   A   U   D   SD

13. Some books should be marked "for class use only" so they will be used with the guidance of a teacher.   SA   A   U   D   SD

14. School librarians should be especially watchful to see that books containing unorthodox views are kept from secondary school library collections.   SA   A   U   D   SD

15. Secondary school librarians should avoid purchasing books that might arouse local critics.   SA   A   U   D   SD

16. Secondary school librarians should not exclude materials because of the origin, background, or views of the authors.   SA   A   U   D   SD

17. Since secondary school librarians are in a position to recognize dangerous ideas in books and other printed materials, they should carefully control their circulation to students.   SA A U D SD

18. Secondary school librarians should avoid purchasing works of fiction dealing with social, psychological, and sexual problems and concentrate more on building collections of classics.   SA A U D SD

19. Secondary school librarians should not purchase conservative publications such as the *Moral Majority Newsletter* and *Conservative Digest*.   SA A U D SD

20. The procedure for dealing with challenged resources should be followed even if a teacher wants a book removed from the secondary school library.   SA A U D SD

21. Secondary school librarians should provide books and other materials presenting a variety of points of view on current and historic issues.   SA A U D SD

22. A censorship controversy over a single book or magazine is not worth the adverse publicity that it could cause for the school.   SA A U D SD

23. Secondary school students should have the freedom to read and consider a wider range of ideas than those that may be held by the majority in the community.   SA A U D SD

24. If the principal requests that a book be removed from the secondary school library, the librarian should remove the book.   SA A U D SD

25. A secondary school library is no place for either conservative or liberal extremist political literature.   SA A U D SD

26. Books about controversial subjects should be starred as a guide for students who wish to avoid works of this type.   SA A U D SD

27. Secondary school librarians, as guardians of the students' freedom to read, should resist efforts of individuals or groups seeking to impose their views upon the school library.
SA   A   U   D   SD

28. Secondary school students need to have access to a variety of resources to help to develop critical thinking skills.
SA   A   U   D   SD

29. Controversial books in secondary school libraries should be kept on restricted shelves.
SA   A   U   D   SD

30. Secondary school librarians should be vigorous advocates of intellectual freedom.
SA   A   U   D   SD

31. If a secondary school librarian has ordered a controversial but positively reviewed book, and now the book is the object of court action in another school in the state, the librarian should cancel the order.
SA   A   U   D   SD

32. It is the responsibility of librarians to give full meaning to the freedom to read by providing books that enrich the quality of thought and expression.
SA   A   U   D   SD

33. Secondary school librarians should not purchase books which might offend the school principal.
SA   A   U   D   SD

34. Secondary school librarians should make it possible for students to choose freely from a variety of points of view on controversial subjects.
SA   A   U   D   SD

35. Secondary school librarians need not endorse every idea in the books they make available.
SA   A   U   D   SD

36. Secondary school librarians have a responsibility to see that school policies about selection and reevaluation of resources are followed.
SA   A   U   D   SD

37. Some issues, such as homosexuality, are just too controversial for a secondary school library.
SA   A   U   D   SD

38. Students should not use interlibrary   SA   A   U   D   SD
loan to acquire books that the librarian has
determined are not appropriate for the
secondary school library collection.

39. Parents should be able to expect that   SA   A   U   D   SD
the books in a secondary school library will
not undermine their family values.

40. Secondary school librarians should   SA   A   U   D   SD
make available the widest diversity of views
and expressions, including those which are
unpopular with the majority.

41. Secondary school librarians should not   SA   A   U   D   SD
select books that present our government
in an unfavorable light.

SECTION III. OPINIONS ABOUT SOCIAL PROBLEMS

This questionnaire is aimed at understanding how people think about social problems. Different people often have different opinions about questions of right and wrong. There are no "right" answers in the way that there are right answers to math problems. We would like you to tell us what you think about several problem stories. The papers will be fed to a computer to find the average for the whole group, and no one will see your individual answers.

Here is a story as an example.

> Frank Jones has been thinking about buying a car. He is married, has two small children and earns an average income. The car he buys will be his family's only car. It will be used mostly to get to work and drive around town, but sometimes for vacation trips also. In trying to decide what car to buy, Frank Jones realized that there were a lot of questions to consider. Below there is a list of some of these questions.

If you were Frank Jones, how important would each of these questions be in deciding what car to buy?

Instructions for Part A: (Sample Question)
On the left hand side check one of the spaces by each
statement of a consideration. (For instance, if you think that
statement no.1 is not important in making a decision about
buying a car, check the space on the right.)

IMPORTANCE:
Great Much Some Little No

1. Whether the car dealer was in the same block as where Frank lives. (Note that in this sample, the person taking the questionnaire did not think this was important in making a decision.)
2. Would a used car be more economical in the long run than a new car. (Note that a check was put in the far left space to indicate the opinion that this is an important issue in making a decision about buying a car.)
3. Whether the color was green, Frank's favorite color.
4. Whether the cubic inch displacement was at least 200. (Note that if you are unsure about what "cubic inch displacement" means, then mark it "no importance.")
5. Would a large, roomy car be better than a compact car?
6. Whether the front connibilies were differential. (Note that if a statement sounds like gibberish or nonsense to you, mark it "no importance.")

Instructions for Part B: (Sample Question)
From the list of questions above, select the most important
one of the whole group. Put the number of the most
important question on the top line below. Do likewise for
your 2nd, 3rd and 4th most important choices. (Note that the
top choices in this case will come from the statements that
were checked on the far left-hand side—statements #2 and
#5 were thought to be very important. In deciding what is the
most important, a person would re-read #2 and #5, and then
pick one of them as the *most* important, then put the other one
as "second most important," and so on.)

Most	*Second Most* *Important*	*Third Most* *Important*	*Fourth Most* *Important*
5	2	3	1

Heinz And The Drug

In Europe a woman was near death from a special kind of cancer. There was one drug that the doctors thought might save her. It was a form of radium that the druggist in the same town had recently discovered. The drug was expensive to make, and the druggist was charging ten times what the drug cost to make. He paid $200 for the radium and charged $2000 for a small dose of the drug. The sick woman's husband, Heinz, went to everyone he knew to borrow the money, but he could get together only about $1000, which is half of what it cost. He told the druggist that his wife was dying, and asked him to sell it cheaper or let him pay later. But the druggist said, "No, I discovered the drug and I'm going to make money from it." So Heinz got desperate and began to think about breaking into the man's store to steal the drug for his wife.

Should Heinz steal the drug? (Check one)
____ Should steal it   ____ Can't decide
____ Should not steal it

IMPORTANCE:

Great	Much	Some	Little	No

1. Whether a community's laws are going to be upheld.
2. Isn't it only natural for a loving husband to care so much for his wife that he'd steal?
3. Is Heinz willing to risk getting shot as a

burglar or going to jail for the chance that stealing the drug might help?

4. Whether Heinz is a professional wrestler, or has considerable influence with professional wrestlers.
5. Whether Heinz is stealing for himself or doing this solely to help someone else.
6. Whether the druggist's rights to his invention have to be respected.
7. Whether the essence of living is more encompassing than the termination of dying, socially and individually.
8. What values are going to be the basis for governing how people act toward each other.
9. Whether the druggist is going to be allowed to hide behind a worthless law which only protects the rich anyway.
10. Whether the law in this case is getting in the way of the most basic claim of any member of society.
11. Whether the druggist deserves to be robbed for being so greedy and cruel.
12. Would stealing in such a case bring about more total good for the whole society or not.

From the list of questions above, select the four most important:
Most Important _____
Second Most Important _____
Third Most Important _____
Fourth Most Important _____

Student Take-Over

At Harvard University a group of students, called the Students for a Democratic Society (SDS), believe that the University should not have an army ROTC program. SDS students are against the war in Viet Nam, and the army training program helps send men to fight in Viet Nam. The SDS students demanded that Harvard end the army ROTC training program as a university course. This would mean that Harvard students could not get army training as part of their regular course work and not get credit for it towards their degrees.

Agreeing with the SDS students, the Harvard professors voted to end the ROTC program as a university course. But the President of the University stated that he wanted to keep the army program on campus as a course. The SDS students felt that the President was not going to pay attention to the faculty vote or to their demands.

So, one day last April, two hundred SDS students walked into the university's administration building, and told everyone else to get out. They said they were doing this to force Harvard to get rid of the army training program as a course.

Should the students have taken over the administration building? (Check one)

_____ Yes, they should take it over   _____ Can't decide
_____ No, they shouldn't take it over

IMPORTANCE:

Great	Much	Some	Little	No

1. Are the students doing this to really help other people or are they doing it just for kicks?
2. Do the students have any right to take over property that doesn't belong to them?
3. Do the students realize that they might be arrested and fined, and even expelled from school?
4. Would taking over the building in the long run benefit more people to a greater extent?
5. Whether the president stayed within the limits of his authority in ignoring the faculty vote.
6. Will the takeover anger the public and give all students a bad name?
7. Is taking over a building consistent with principles of justice?
8. Would allowing one student take-over encourage many other student take-overs?

<table>
<tr><td></td><td></td><td></td><td></td><td></td></tr>
<tr><td></td><td></td><td></td><td></td><td></td></tr>
<tr><td></td><td></td><td></td><td></td><td></td></tr>
<tr><td></td><td></td><td></td><td></td><td></td></tr>
</table>

9. Did the president bring this misunderstanding on himself by being so unreasonable and uncooperative?
10. Whether running the university ought to be in the hands of a few administrators or in the hands of all the people.
11. Are the students following principles which they believe are above the law?
12. Whether or not university decisions ought to be respected by students.

From the list of questions above, select the four most important:

Most Important _____
Second Most Important _____
Third Most Important _____
Fourth Most Important _____

Escaped Prisoner

A man had been sentenced to prison for 10 years. After one year, however, he escaped from prison, moved to a new area of the country, and took on the name of Thompson. For 8 years he worked hard, and gradually he saved enough money to buy his own business. He was fair to his customers, gave his employees top wages, and gave most of his own profits to charity. Then one day, Mrs. Jones, an old neighbor, recognized him as the man who had escaped from prison 8 years before, and whom the police had been looking for.

Should Mrs. Jones report Mr. Thompson to the police and have him sent back to prison? (Check one)

_____ Should report him   _____ Can't decide
_____ Should not report him

IMPORTANCE:
Great Much Some Little No

1. Hasn't Mr. Thompson been good enough for such a long time to prove he isn't a bad person?

2. Every time someone escapes punishment for a crime, doesn't that just encourage more crime?
3. Wouldn't we be better off without prisons and the oppression of our legal system?
4. Has Mr. Thompson really paid his debt to society?
5. Would society be failing what Mr. Thompson should fairly expect?
6. What benefits would prisons be apart from society, especially for a charitable man?
7. How could anyone be so cruel and heartless as to send Mr. Thompson to prison?
8. Would it be fair to all the prisoners who had to serve out their full sentences if Mr. Thompson was let off?
9. Was Mrs. Jones a good friend of Mr. Thompson?
10. Wouldn't it be a citizen's duty to report an escaped criminal, regardless of the circumstances?
11. How would the will of the people and the public good best be served?
12. Would going to prison do any good for Mr. Thompson or protect anybody?

From the list of questions above, select the four most important:

Most Important _____
Second Most Important _____
Third Most Important _____
Fourth Most Important _____

The Doctor's Dilemma

A lady was dying of cancer which could not be cured and she had only about six months to live. She was in terrible pain, but she was so weak that a good dose of pain-killer like morphine would make her die sooner. She was delirious and almost crazy with pain, and in her calm periods, she would ask the doctor to give her enough morphine to kill her. She said she couldn't stand the pain and that she was going to die in a few months anyway.

What should the doctor do? (Check one)

_____ He should give the lady an _____ Can't decide
overdose that will make her die
_____ Should not give the overdose

IMPORTANCE:

Great	Much	Some	Little	No	
					1. Whether the woman's family is in favor of giving her the overdose or not.
					2. Is the doctor obligated by the same laws as everybody else if giving her an overdose would be the same as killing her?
					3. Whether people would be much better off without society regimenting their lives and even their deaths.
					4. Whether the doctor could make it appear like an accident.
					5. Does the state have the right to force continued existence on those who don't want to live?
					6. What is the value of death prior to society's perspective on personal values?
					7. Whether the doctor has sympathy for the woman's suffering or cares more about what society might think.
					8. Is helping to end another's life ever a responsible act of cooperation?
					9. Whether only God should decide when a person's life should end.
					10. What values the doctor has set for himself in his own personal code of behavior.
					11. Can society afford to let everybody end their lives when they want to?
					12. Can society allow suicides or mercy killing and still protect the lives of individuals who want to live?

From the list of questions above,
select the four most important:
Most Important _____
Second Most Important _____
Third Most Important _____
Fourth Most Important _____

Webster

Mr. Webster was the owner and manager of a gas station. He wanted to hire another mechanic to help him, but good mechanics were hard to find. The only person he found who seemed to be a good mechanic was Mr. Lee, but he was Chinese. While Mr. Webster himself didn't have anything against Orientals, he was afraid to hire Mr. Lee because many of his customers didn't like Orientals. His customers might take their business elsewhere if Mr. Lee was working in the gas station.

When Mr. Lee asked Mr. Webster if he could have the job, Mr. Webster said that he had already hired somebody else. But Mr. Webster really had not hired anybody, because he could not find anybody who was a good mechanic besides Mr. Lee.

What should Mr. Webster have done? (Check one)

_____ Should have hired Mr. Lee   _____ Can't decide
_____ Should not have hired him

IMPORTANCE:

Great	Much	Some	Little	No

1. Does the owner of a business have the right to make his own business decisions or not?
2. Whether there is a law that forbids racial discrimination in hiring for jobs.
3. Whether Mr. Webster is prejudiced against Orientals himself or whether he means nothing personal in refusing the job.
4. Whether hiring a good mechanic or paying attention to his customers' wishes would be best for his business.
5. What individual differences ought to be relevant in deciding how society's roles are filled?
6. Whether the greedy and competitive capitalistic system ought to be completely abandoned.

7. Do a majority of people in Mr. Webster's society feel like his customers or are a majority against prejudice?
8. Whether hiring capable men like Mr. Lee would use talents that would otherwise be lost to society.
9. Would refusing the job to Mr. Lee be consistent with Mr. Webster's own moral beliefs?
10. Could Mr. Webster be so hard-hearted as to refuse the job, knowing how much it means to Mr. Lee?
11. Whether the Christian commandment to love your fellow man applies to this case.
12. If someone's in need, shouldn't he be helped regardless of what you get back from him?

From the list of questions above, select the four most important:

Most Important ____
Second Most Important ____
Third Most Important ____
Fourth Most Important ____

Newspaper

Fred, a senior in high school, wanted to publish a mimeographed newspaper for students so that he could express many of his opinions. He wanted to speak out against the war in Viet Nam and to speak out against some of the school's rules, like the rule forbidding boys to wear long hair.

When Fred started his newspaper, he asked his principal for permission. The principal said it would be all right if before every publication Fred would turn in all his articles for the principal's approval. Fred agreed and turned in several articles for approval. The principal approved all of them and Fred published two issues of the paper in the next two weeks.

But the principal had not expected that Fred's newspaper would receive so much attention. Students were so excited by the paper that they began to organize protests against the hair regulation and other school rules. Angry parents objected to Fred's opinions. They phoned the principal telling him that the newspaper was unpatriotic and should not be published. As a result of the rising excitement, the principal ordered Fred to stop publishing. He gave as a reason that Fred's activities were disruptive to the operation of the school.

Should the principal stop the newspaper? (Check one)

____ Should stop it   ____ Can't decide

____ Should not stop it

IMPORTANCE:

Great	Much	Some	Little	No

1. Is the principal more responsible to students or to the parents?
2. Did the principal give his word that the newspaper could be published for a long time, or did he just promise to approve the newspaper one issue at a time?
3. Would the students start protesting even more if the principal stopped the newspaper?
4. When the welfare of the school is threatened, does the principal have the right to give orders to students?
5. Does the principal have the freedom of speech to say "no" in this case?
6. If the principal stopped the newspaper would he be preventing full discussion of important problems?
7. Whether the principal's order would make Fred lose faith in the principal.
8. Whether Fred was really loyal to his school and patriotic to his country.
9. What effect would stopping the paper have on the student's education in critical thinking and judgments?
10. Whether Fred was in any way violating the rights of others in publishing his own opinions.
11. Whether the principal should be influenced by some angry parents when it is the principal who knows best what is going on in the school.
12. Whether Fred was using the newspaper to stir up hatred and discontent.

From the list of questions above,
select the four most important:
Most Important _____
Second Most Important _____
Third Most Important _____
Fourth Most Important _____

DIT reprinted with permission

Letters of Transmittal

Survey of Secondary School Librarians

Dear Secondary School Librarian/Media Specialist,

Recent judicial decisions in Tennessee and Alabama have focused attention on the use of resources in schools. Although school librarians have major concerns about resources, there is no current information available which describes the opinions of secondary school librarians about resources in schools. This survey affords an opportunity for secondary school librarians to voice their opinions about a variety of school library and related issues.

This research is part of my doctoral program at the University of Minnesota and the survey is an important part of my dissertation. But, I know that school librarians are especially busy at the end of a school year. However, I am confident that you will understand the importance of this research to both of us and will take the time to complete the enclosed survey.

Your responses are essential. You are one of a limited number of secondary school librarians in Minnesota, Iowa, and Wisconsin receiving this survey. Therefore, your individual response is needed to obtain a representative picture of the opinions of librarians in your state.

A Note on Privacy:

> I am vitally concerned about the importance of protecting your privacy. You will notice a sequence number on your survey form. This sequence number will be used only to be sure you are not bothered by reminder letters once you have completed and returned your survey.

174

Information which you provide will be combined with information from other librarians in Minnesota, Wisconsin, and Iowa. At no time will your name or school district be identified.

If you have questions about this survey, please call me at (507) 931–1956. Please complete your survey within one week. For your convenience, I have provided a pre-addressed, postage-paid envelope. Please use it to return your completed survey. Thank you in advance for your cooperation.

Sincerely yours,

Frances Beck McDonald
Graduate Student
University of Minnesota

Survey of Secondary School Librarians

Dear Secondary School Librarian/Media Specialist:

All of us are busier these days than we should be, and most of us have a hard time keeping up with essential day to day duties and obligations. I know that extra requests receive our best intentions, but I also know that in reality few of us have the time that we need to fulfill these intentions.

Two weeks ago, you received a school library and social issues survey. As of this date, May 17, I have not received a completed survey from you. Perhaps you mislaid the survey or it may have miscarried in the mail—any of a number of contingencies could have happened.

In the event you did not receive the survey, I am enclosing another copy for you. I am sure that you will try to find from thirty to forty-five minutes in your busy schedule to complete the survey and drop it in the nearest mailbox.

If the results of the study are to be as accurate as possible, each individual response to all parts of the survey is necessary. Your opinions are an important part of the information needed from school librarians in your state.

Thank you. I shall appreciate your kindness.

Sincerely yours,

Frances Beck McDonald
Graduate Student
University of Minnesota

Survey of Secondary School Librarians

Dear Secondary School Librarian/Media Specialist:

At the end of the school year, you received a school library and social issues survey from me. Although many media specialists in your state have returned their completed surveys I still do not have a response from you. Your opinions are still needed.

Perhaps without the pressures all media people experience during the school year, you will now be able to find the time to complete the survey and return it to me in the enclosed envelope on which I have placed postage for your convenience.

In case you left the previous survey at school, I am sending another copy to you.

Please take the time to complete all parts of the survey for me. I am anxious to complete my research and I would not like to bother you with another reminder once the school year begins.

Thank you for your time. I truly appreciate your cooperation.

Sincerely yours,

Frances Beck McDonald
Graduate Student
University of Minnesota

Judges' Rating Form

Intellectual Freedom/Censorship Attitude Survey

Directions for Judges:

1. On the line below each statement, *write* the *descriptor* of the Intellectual Freedom or Censorship concept being addressed. Some concepts may overlap; in such cases write the most obvious on the line and the other(s) below.

Descriptors	*Concepts*
Diversity	Providing resources representing a variety of issues and points of view
Access	Providing equal access to resources for all users of a library
Controversy	Providing resources about issues which might be considered by some to be controversial
Selection	Using criteria for selecting resources: personal, educational, community values, other
Policy	Following policies and procedures when resources are challenged
Profession	Exercising professional values and beliefs related to intellectual freedom and censorship
Other	Please name

2. Circle the number which indicates the strength of the statement. Circle 6 if an item is not clear. Suggest alternate wording, if you like.

1	2	3	4	5	6
Strongly descriptive of Intellectual Freedom	Somewhat descriptive of Intellectual Freedom	Somewhat neutral	Somewhat descriptive of Censorship	Strongly descriptive of Censorship	Item not clear

Example:
The rights of an individual to use the school library should not be denied because of origin, age, background or views.

<u>Profession</u>   1   2   3   4   5   6
Descriptor

PLEASE DO NOT LET YOUR PERSONAL AGREEMENT OR DISAGREEMENT WITH THE CONTENT OF THE ITEM INFLUENCE YOUR SCORING.

Rt. 1 Box 173
Kasota, Minnesota 56050

Dear Intellectual Freedom Advocate:

As part of my doctoral program at the University of Minnesota, I am doing research in the area of intellectual freedom. To complete my study, I need your help. I must develop a questionnaire to measure the attitudes of secondary school librarians toward intellectual freedom and censorship. You have been asked for help because of your reputation and expertise in the area of intellectual freedom and/or because as a media educator, you are teaching these concepts to your students.

The process of developing the questionnaire involves enlisting the aid of experts like you to determine which of many potential survey items represent the strongest statements illustrating either intellectual freedom or censorship. Your task involves rating the strength of the statements so that weak statements may be eliminated and the questionnaire be of reasonable length, but still provide the strongest measure possible. Further, to ensure that the questionnaire addresses all aspects of intellectual freedom and censorship important in secondary school libraries, you are being asked to identify the intellectual freedom concepts being addressed.

I know that you are extremely busy. I also know that completing a form of this length and complexity represents a considerable contribution on your part. However, because of your commitment to intellectual freedom, I am hoping that you will participate with me in the development of this attitude survey instrument. Although I am unable to compensate you for your efforts, the results of the study should provide information to persons working to preserve freedom to read in our schools as well as a validated survey instrument which might be useful for subsequent research.

Because time is always a problem for graduate students, I would be grateful if you could return your survey in the enclosed stamped, self-addressed envelope as soon as possible, and no later than March 9, 1987.

I appreciate your willingness to help me to complete my research. Thank you for continuing your contribution to the cause of intellectual freedom.

Sincerely,

Frances M. McDonald

INTELLECTUAL FREEDOM/CENSORSHIP
ATTITUDE SCALE FREQUENCIES

Intellectual Freedom/Censorship Attitude Scale Frequencies

Scale Items	SA	A	U	D	SD
12. The secondary school librarian's moral and aesthetic values should be the standard for determining what books should be included in the school library collection.	9 (2.8)	20 (6.1)	14 (4.3)	161 (49.2)	123 (37.6)
13. Some books should be marked "for class use only" so they will be used with the guidance of a teacher.	5 (1.5)	61 (18.7)	44 (13.5)	136 (41.6)	81 (24.8)
14. School librarians should be especially watchful to see that books containing unorthodox views are kept from secondary school library collections.	0 (0)	9 (2.7)	18 (5.5)	128 (39.0)	173 (52.7)
15. Secondary school librarians should avoid purchasing books that might arouse local critics.	1 (.3)	19 (5.8)	29 (8.8)	173 (52.7)	106 (32.3)
16. Secondary school librarians should not exclude materials because of the origin, background or views of the authors.	138 (42.1)	147 (44.8)	10 (3.0)	19 (5.8)	14 (4.3)
17. Since secondary school librarians are in a position to recognize dangerous ideas in books and other printed materials, they should carefully control their circulation to students.	2 (.6)	22 (6.7)	33 (10.1)	137 (41.9)	133 (40.7)

Scale Items	SA	A	U	D	SD
18. Secondary school librarians should avoid purchasing works of fiction dealing with social, psychological, and sexual problems and concentrate more on building collections of classics.	0 (0)	1 (.3)	6 (1.8)	154 (47.0)	167 (50.9)
19. Secondary school librarians should not purchase conservative publications such as the *Moral Majority Newsletter* and *Conservative Digest*.	1 (.3)	21 (6.4)	64 (19.5)	186 (56.7)	56 (17.1)
20. The procedure for dealing with challenged resources should be followed even if a teacher wants a book removed from the secondary school library.	163 (49.8)	154 (47.1)	7 (2.1)	0 (0)	3 (.9)
21. Secondary school librarians should provide books and other materials presenting a variety of points of view on current and historic issues.	242 (73.8)	85 (25.9)	0 (0)	0 (0)	1 (.3)
22. A censorship controversy over a single book or magazine is not worth the adverse publicity that it could cause for the school.	5 (1.5)	28 (8.5)	68 (20.7)	136 (41.5)	91 (27.7)
23. Secondary school students should have the freedom to read and consider a wider range of ideas than those that may be held by the majority in the community.	152 (46.3)	165 (50.3)	6 (1.8)	5 (1.5)	0 (0)
24. If the principal requests that a book be removed from the secondary school library, the librarian should remove the book.	2 (.6)	40 (12.2)	49 (14.9)	141 (43.0)	96 (29.3)

Scale Items	SA	A	U	D	SD
25. A secondary school library is no place for either conservative or liberal extremist political literature.	3 (0.9)	17 (5.2)	46 (14.0)	185 (56.4)	77 (23.5)
26. Books about controversial subjects should be starred as a guide for students who wish to avoid works of this type.	0 (0)	10 (3.0)	30 (9.1)	182 (55.5)	106 (32.3)
27. Secondary school librarians, as guardians of the students' freedom to read, should resist efforts of individuals or groups seeking to impose their views upon the school library.	148 (45.1)	151 (46.0)	13 (4.0)	15 (4.6)	1 (.3)
28. Secondary school students need to have access to a variety of resources to help to develop critical thinking skills.	216 (65.9)	112 (34.1)	0 (0.0)	0 (0.0)	0 (0.0)
29. Controversial books in secondary school libraries should be kept on restricted shelves.	1 (.3)	22 (6.7)	30 (9.1)	160 (48.8)	115 (35.1)
30. Secondary school librarians should be vigorous advocates of intellectual freedom.	168 (51.2)	137 (41.8)	17 (5.2)	6 (1.8)	0 (0)
31. If a secondary school librarian has ordered a controversial but positively reviewed book, and now that book is the object of court action in another school in the state, the librarian should cancel the order.	1 (.3)	8 (2.4)	25 (7.6)	187 (57.0)	107 (32.6)
32. It is the responsibility of librarians to give full meaning to the freedom to read by providing books that enrich the quality of thought and expression.	176 (53.7)	148 (45.1)	3 (.9)	1 (.3)	0 (0)

Scale Items	SA	A	U	D	SD
33. Secondary school librarians should not purchase books which might offend the school principal.	1 (.3)	9 (2.7)	19 (5.8)	188 (57.3)	111 (33.8)
34. Secondary school librarians should make it possible for students to choose freely from a variety of points of view on controversial subjects.	167 (50.9)	158 (48.2)	2 (0.6)	1 (0.3)	0 (0.0)
35. Secondary school librarians need not endorse every idea in the books they make available.	184 (56.1)	140 (42.7)	1 (0.3)	3 (0.9)	0 (0.0)
36. Secondary school librarians have a responsibility to see that school policies about selection and reevaluation of resources are followed.	180 (54.9)	144 (43.9)	4 (1.2)	0 (0.0)	0 (0.0)
37. Some issues, such as homosexuality, are just too controversial for a secondary school library.	1 (.3)	5 (1.5)	11 (3.4)	177 (54.0)	134 (40.9)
38. Students should not use interlibrary loan to acquire books that the librarian has determined are not appropriate for the secondary school library collection.	1 (.3)	10 (3.0)	41 (12.5)	174 (53.0)	102 (31.1)
39. Parents should be able to expect that the books in a secondary school library will not undermine their family values.	7 (2.1)	75 (22.9)	78 (23.9)	136 (41.6)	31 (9.5)

Scale Items	SA	A	U	D	SD
40. Secondary school librarians should make available the widest diversity of views and expressions, including those which are unpopular with the majority.	97 (29.6)	205 (62.5)	20 (6.1)	5 (1.5)	1 (0.3)
41. Secondary school librarians should not select books that present our government in an unfavorable light.	5 (1.5)	21 (6.4)	36 (11.0)	198 (60.4)	68 (20.7)

INTELLECTUAL FREEDOM/CENSORSHIP
ATTITUDE SCALE CORRELATIONS
WITH SCALE SUMS

Intellectual Freedom/Censorship Attitude Scale Correlations with Scale Sums

Scale Item	r (IF)	r (C)	r (IFC)
12. The secondary school librarian's moral and aesthetic values should be the standard for determining what books should be included in the school library collection.	.3142**	.5853	.5405
13. Some books should be marked "for class use only" so they will be used with the guidance of a teacher.	.3592	.6165	.5778
14. School librarians should be especially watchful to see that books containing unorthodox views are kept from secondary school library collections.	.5224	.7155	.7031
15. Secondary school librarians should avoid purchasing books that might arouse local critics.	.5042	.7518	.7253
16. Secondary school librarians should not exclude materials because of the origin, background, or views of the authors.	−.5620	−.2886	−.3977
17. Since secondary school librarians are in a position to recognize dangerous ideas in books and other printed materials, they should carefully control their circulation to students.	.4583	.7688	.7238
18. Secondary school librarians should avoid purchasing works of fiction dealing with social, psychological, and sexual problems and concentrate more on building collections of classics.	.5618	.5833	.6156

Scale Item	r (IF)	r (C)	r (IFC)
19. Secondary school librarians should not purchase conservative publications such as the *Moral Majority Newsletter* and *Conservative Digest*.	.3099	.5002	.4742
20. The procedure for dealing with challenged resources should be followed even if a teacher wants a book removed from the secondary school library.	−.4658	−.4749	−.5052
21. Secondary school librarians should provide books and other materials presenting a variety of points of view on current and historic issues.	−.5830	−.4400	−.5147
22. A censorship controversy over a single book or magazine is not worth the adverse publicity that it could cause for the school.	.4671	.7257	.6950
23. Secondary school students should have the freedom to read and consider a wider range of ideas than those that may be held by the majority in the community.	−.6836	−.4980	−.5909
24. If the principal requests that a book be removed from the secondary school library, the librarian should remove the book.	.4945	.7458	.7179
25. A secondary school library is no place for either conservative or liberal extremist political literature.	.4280	.6045	.5931
26. Books about controversial subjects should be starred as a guide for students who wish to avoid works of this type.	.3597	.6157	.5806

Scale Item	r (IF)	r (C)	r (IFC)
27. Secondary school librarians, as guardians of the students' freedom to read, should resist efforts of individuals or groups seeking to impose their views upon the school library.	−.6921	−.5282	−.6165
28. Secondary school students need to have access to a variety of resources to help to develop critical thinking skills.	−.6448	−.5134	−.5902
29. Controversial books in secondary school libraries should be kept on restricted shelves.	.4932	.7089	.6893
30. Secondary school librarians should be vigorous advocates of intellectual freedom.	−.7127	−.4948	−.5964
31. If a secondary school librarian has ordered a controversial but positively reviewed book, and now that book is the object of court action in another school in the state, the librarian should cancel the order.	.5731	.7348	.7351
32. It is the responsibility of librarians to give full meaning to the freedom to read by providing books that enrich the quality of thought and expression.	−.6975	−.4683	−.5735
33. Secondary school librarians should not purchase books which might offend the school principal.	.5478	.6839	.6881
34. Secondary school librarians should make it possible for students to choose freely from a variety of points of view on controversial subjects.	−.7439	−.5790	−.6713

Scale Item	r (IF)	r (C)	r (IFC)
35. Secondary school librarians need not endorse every idea in the books they make available.	−.6394	−.4329	−.5312
36. Secondary school librarians have a responsibility to see that school policies about selection and reevaluation of resources are followed.	−.6097	−.4080	−.5024
37. Some issues, such as homosexuality, are just too controversial for a secondary school library.	.5547	.6263	.6479
38. Students should not use interlibrary loan to acquire books that the librarian has determined are not appropriate for the secondary school library collection.	.3878	.5532	.5396
39. Parents should be able to expect that the books in a secondary school library will not undermine their family values.	.3145	.5234	.4931
40. Secondary school librarians should make available the widest diversity of views and expressions, including those which are unpopular with the majority.	−.6818	−.5331	−.6163
41. Secondary school librarians should not select books that present our government in an unfavorable light.	.4546	.7068	.6755

APPENDIX F

ANALYSIS OF VARIANCE

Analysis of Variance
Intellectual Freedom Attitude Scores

Intellectual Freedom Scores and State

	df	ss	x̄ squares	f ratio	f prob
Between groups	2	31.1445	15.5723	.8924	.4107
Within groups	325	5671.5110	17.4508		
Total	327	5702.6555			

Intellectual Freedom Scores and Size of School

	df	ss	x̄ squares	f ratio	f prob
Between groups	5	399.5166	79.9033	4.8399	.0003
Within groups	318	5249.9988	16.5094		
Total	323	5649.5154			

Intellectual Freedom Scores and Grades in School

	df	ss	x̄ squares	f ratio	f prob
Between groups	5	155.4457	31.0891	1.8046	.1115
Within groups	322	5547.2098	17.2274		
Total	327	5702.6555			

Intellectual Freedom Scores and Age

	df	ss	x̄ squares	f ratio	f prob
Between groups	4	56.1764	14.0441	.8021	.5245
Within groups	318	5567.7121	17.5085		
Total	322	5623.8885			

Intellectual Freedom Scores and Years Experience

	df	ss	x̄ squares	f ratio	f prob
Between groups	4	154.0991	38.5248	2.2489	.0637
Within groups	322	5516.1272	17.1308		
Total	326	5670.2263			

Intellectual Freedom Scores and Level of Education

	df	ss	x̄ squares	f ratio	f prob
Between groups	4	570.9927	142.7482	9.0747	.0000
Within groups	321	5049.4398	15.7303		
Total	325	5620.4325			

df = degrees of freedom; ss = sum of the squares; x̄ squares = mean; f ratio = ratio of between-group variance to within-group variance; f prob = observed significance level

Censorship Attitude Scores

Censorship Scores and State

	df	ss	x̄ squares	f ratio	f prob
Between groups	2	509.4629	254.7315	2.4805	.0853
Within groups	320	32861.6021	102.6925		
Total	322	33371.0650			

Censorship Scores and Size of School

	df	ss	x̄ squares	f ratio	f prob
Between groups	5	3215.2959	643.0592	6.7526	.0000
Within groups	313	29807.4502	95.2315		
Total	318	33022.7461			

Censorship Scores and Grades in School

	df	ss	x̄ squares	f ratio	f prob
Between groups	5	1501.91225	300.3824	2.9879	.0119
Within groups	317	31869.1528	100.5336		
Total	322	33371.0650			

Censorship Scores and Level of Education

	df	ss	x̄ squares	f ratio	f prob
Between groups	4	3504.6296	876.1574	9.3611	.0000
Within groups	316	29576.1803	93.5955		
Total	320	33080.8100			

Censorship Scores and Age

	df	ss	x̄ squares	f ratio	f prob
Between groups	4	435.2768	109.8192	1.0663	.3733
Within groups	313	32236.7766	102.9929		
Total	317	32676.0535			

Censorship Scores and Years of Experience

	df	ss	x̄ squares	f ratio	f prob
Between groups	4	729.1379	182.2845	1.7794	.1327
Within groups	317	32474.4149	102.4429		
Total	321	33203.5528			

Intellectual Freedom/Censorship Scores

Intellectual Freedom/Censorship Scores and State

	df	ss	x̄ squares	f ratio	f prob
Between groups	2	760.0611	380.0305	2.1229	.1214
Within groups	320	57284.1742	179.0130		
Total	322	58044.2353			

Intellectual Freedom/Censorship Scores and Size of School

	df	ss	x̄ squares	f ratio	f prob
Between groups	5	5688.5790	1137.7158	6.8761	.0000
Within groups	313	51788.9634	165.4599		
Total	318	57477.5423			

Intellectual Freedom/Censorship Scores and Grades in School

	df	ss	x̄ squares	f ratio	f prob
Between groups	5	2228.0335	445.6067	2.5308	.0289
Within groups	317	55816.2018	176.0763		
Total	322	58044.2353			

Intellectual Freedom/Censorship Scores and Years of Experience

	df	ss	x̄ squares	f ratio	f prob
Between groups	4	1413.0202	353.2551	1.9896	.0959
Within groups	317	56284.6195	177.5540		
Total	321	57697.6398			

Intellectual Freedom/Censorship Scores and Age

	df	ss	x̄ squares	f ratio	f prob
Between groups	4	649.5927	162.3982	.9049	.4613
Within groups	316	56169.9041	179.4566		
Total	317	56819.4969			

Intellectual Freedom/Censorship Scores and Level of Education

	df	ss	x̄ squares	f ratio	f prob
Between groups	4	6829.1158	1707.2789	10.6207	.0000
Within groups	316	50796.9091	160.7497		
Total	320	57626.0249			

Institution of Educational Preparation

Intellectual Freedom Scores and Institution of Educational Preparation

	df	ss	x̄ squares	f ratio	f prob
Between groups	2	165.5387	82.7693	4.8581	.0083
Within groups	325	5537.1168	17.0373		
Total	327	5702.6555			

Censorship Scores and Institution of Educational Preparation

	df	ss	x̄ squares	f ratio	f prob
Between groups	2	753.0322	376.5161	3.6938	.0259
Within groups	320	32618.0328	101.9314		
Total	322	33371.0650			

APPENDIX G

MEAN DIFFERENCES

Mean Differences by State

State	IF Mean	C Mean	Mean Dif	Categories			
				Policy	Diversity	Access	Selection
MN	4.4364	4.1239	.3174	.4500	.2667	.3518	.2189
IA	4.3907	4.0171	.3790	.4346	.2695	.5383	.3061
WI	4.4658	4.1674	.2968	.3859	.2688	.3459	.1929

Mean Differences by School Size

Size of School	IF Mean	C Mean	Mean Dif	Categories			
				Policy	Diversity	Access	Selection
0–199	4.2571	3.7810	.4762	.7698	.3532	.5524	.3234
200–299	4.3439	3.9183	.4256	.4350	.3537	.5488	.3537
300–499	4.3366	4.0571	.2846	.4391	.1962	.4118	.1743
500–999	4.4624	4.1012	.3607	.4275	.2980	.4035	.3005
1000–1999	4.5907	4.3438	.2521	.3089	.2367	.3173	.1522
2000 +	4.5889	4.1667	.4222	.3333	.3796	.4778	.4352

Mean Differences by Grades in School

Grades	IF Mean	C Mean	Mean Dif	Policy	Diversity	Access	Selection
7–8	4.3750	4.0750	.3000	.4167	.1806	.4083	.2396
7–9	4.3471	4.0559	.2912	.4020	.4461	.1647	.1691
7–12	4.4744	4.0047	.4698	.4903	.3583	.6291	.3857
9–12	4.4615	4.1631	.3005	.4572	.2385	.3312	.2003
10–12	4.5079	4.3431	.1847	.1535	.1601	.2605	.2094
Other	4.3136	4.0231	.2877	.4419	.2323	.4076	.1446

Mean Differences by Level of Education

Education	IF Mean	C Mean	Mean Dif	Policy	Diversity	Access	Selection
BA,BS	4.4500	4.0500	.4000	.3667	.4417	.7500	.0917
BA,BS+	4.2802	3.9056	.3774	.5172	.2626	.4794	.2930
MA,MS	4.4440	4.1720	.2720	.3500	.2883	.3600	.1017
MA,MS+	4.5779	4.2711	.3102	.3830	.2564	.3542	.2576
Spec	4.4667	4.1778	.2889	.2778	.2963	.3222	.2315

Mean Differences by Institution of Educational Preparation

Institut.	IF Mean	C Mean	Mean Dif	Policy	Categories Diversity	Access	Selection
State	4.3948	4.0836	.3129	.3973	.2550	.4112	.2042
Private	4.3437	3.8687	.4750	.6458	.2917	.6125	.4167
ALA	4.5550	4.2115	.3487	.4542	.3021	.3688	.3026

Institut.—Institution
State—State College or University
Private—Private College or University
ALA—ALA Accredited Library School

Mean Differences by ALA Membership

Member	IF Mean	C Mean	Mean Dif	Policy	Categories Diversity	Access	Selection
No	4.4134	4.0832	.3323	.4407	.2697	.4232	.2283
Yes	4.6083	4.3139	.2944	.3333	.2431	.3306	.2581

Mean Differences by AASL Membership

| | IF | C | Mean | | Categories | | |
Member	Mean	Mean	Dif	Policy	Diversity	Access	Selection
No	4.4160	4.0795	.3385	.4485	.2671	.4337	.2371
Yes	4.6094	4.3750	.2344	.2500	.2630	.2251	.1823

Mean Differences by State Membership

| | IF | C | Mean | | Categories | | |
Member	Mean	Mean	Dif	Policy	Diversity	Access	Selection
Yes	4.4786	4.1736	.3099	.4002	.2545	.3460	.2511
No	4.3714	4.0157	.3557	.4548	.2869	.4986	.2217

BIBLIOGRAPHY

Ahrens, Nyla Herber. "Censorship and the Teacher of English: A Questionnaire Survey of a Selected Sample of Secondary School Teachers of English." Doctoral dissertation, Columbia University, 1965.

Allport, Gordon W. "Attitudes." Reprinted in Jahoda, Marie, and Neil Warren, eds. *Attitudes: Selected Readings.* New York: Penguin Books, 1967, 15–21.

Alozie, Chukwuma Francis Ethelbert. "An Analysis of the Interrelationship of Two Measures used in the Measurement of Moral Judgment Development: The Kohlberg Moral Judgment Interview and the Rest Defining Issues Test." Doctoral dissertation, University of Minnesota, 1976.

American Association of School Librarians. *Information Power: Guidelines for School Library Media Programs.* Chicago: American Association of School Librarians and Association for Educational Communications and Technology, 1988.

American Association of School Librarians. *Media Programs: District and School.* Chicago: American Library Association and Association for Educational Communications and Technology, 1975.

American Association of School Librarians. *Standards for School Library Programs.* Chicago: American Library Association, 1960.

American Association of School Librarians. *Standards for School Media Programs.* Chicago and Washington, D.C.: American Library Association and National Education Association, 1969.

American Library Association. *Handbook of Organization.* Chicago: American Library Association, 1988.

American Library Association. *Intellectual Freedom Manual.* 3d ed. Chicago: American Library Association, 1989.

Association of American Publishers. *Limiting What Students Shall Read: Books and Other Learning Materials in Our Public Schools: How They Are Selected and How They Are Removed.* Washington, D.C.: American Association of Publishers, American Library Association, Association for Supervision and Curriculum Development, 1981.

Balian, Edward S. *How to Design, Analyze, and Write Doctoral Research: The Practical Guidebook.* Lanham, Maryland: University Press of America, 1982.

Barnett, Robert, and Joseph M. Volker. "Moral Judgment and Life Experiences." Unpublished manuscript. Minneapolis: University of Minnesota, 1985.

Blasi, Augusto. "Bridging Moral Cognition and Moral Action: A Critical Review of the Literature." *Psychological Bulletin* 88 (July, 1980), 1–45.

Borg, Walter R., and Meredith Damien Gall. *Educational Research: An Introduction.* 4th ed. New York: Longman, 1983.

Broderick, Dorothy. "Adolescent Development and Censorship." In *School Library Media Annual 1983,* Vol. 1. Aaron, Shirley, and Pat Scales, eds. Littleton, Colorado: Libraries Unlimited, 1983, 43–53.

Bump, Myrna Marlene. "Censorship Practiced by High School Librarians Prior to (Actual) Book Selection." Doctoral dissertation, Kansas State University, 1980.

Bundy, Mary Lee, and Teresa Stakem. "Librarians and Intellectual Freedom: Are Opinions Changing?" *Wilson Library Bulletin* 57 (April, 1982), 584–589.

Burress, Lee. "Censorship in School Libraries." *ALA Yearbook 1983.* Chicago: American Library Association, 1983, 246–247.

Burress, Lee. "Censorship in Wisconsin Public High Schools." *How Censorship Affects the School and Other Essays*. Racine: Wisconsin Council of Teachers of English, 1984, 60–101.

Burress, Lee. "Summary Report of a Survey of Censorship Pressures on the American High School, 1982." Urbana, Illinois: National Council of Teachers of English, 1983.

Busha, Charles H. "The Attitudes of Midwestern Public Librarians Toward Intellectual Freedom and Censorship." Doctoral dissertation, Indiana University, 1971.

Busha, Charles H. *Freedom Versus Suppression and Censorship: With a Study of the Attitudes of Midwestern Public Librarians and a Bibliography of Censorship*. Littleton, Colorado: Libraries Unlimited, 1972.

Candee, Daniel. "The Moral Psychology of Watergate and Its Aftermath." In Wilson, Richard W., and Gordon J. Schochet. *Moral Development and Politics*. New York: Praeger, 1980, 172–189.

Colby, Anne, and Lawrence Kohlberg. "Invariant Sequence and Internal Consistency in Moral Judgment Stages." In Kurtines, William M., and Jacob Gewirtz. *Morality, Moral Behavior, and Moral Development*. New York: John Wiley, 1984, 41–51.

Crano, William D., and Marilyn B. Brewer. *Principles and Methods of Social Research*. Boston: Allyn and Bacon, 1986.

Deemer, Deborah K. "Research in Moral Education." Chicago: American Educational Research Association, 1985.

Douma, Rollin. "Censorship in the English Classroom: A Review of Research." *Journal of Research and Development in Education* 9 (1976), 60–68.

Downs, Robert B. "Freedom of Speech and Press: Development of a Concept." *Library Trends* 19 (1970), 8–18.

Downs, Robert B., and Ralph E. McCoy, eds. *The First Freedom Today: Critical Issues Relating to Censorship and Intellectual Freedom*. Chicago: American Library Association, 1984.

England, Claire St Clere. "The Climate of Censorship in Ontario." Doctoral dissertation, University of Toronto, 1974.

Farley, John J. "Book Censorship in the Senior High Libraries of Nassau County, New York." Doctoral dissertation, New York University, 1964.

Fishbein, Martin, and Icek Ajzen. *Belief, Attitude, Intention and Behavior.* Reading, Massachusetts: Addison-Wesley, 1975.

Fiske, Marjorie (Lowenthal). *Book Selection and Censorship: A Study of School and Public Librarians in California.* Berkeley: University of California Press, 1959.

Flagg, Wilma T. "Internal Censorship of Periodicals by Missouri School Librarians in Grades 9–12." Master's thesis, Central Missouri State University, 1986.

Geller, Evelyn. *Forbidden Books in American Public Libraries, 1876–1939: A Study in Cultural Change.* Westport, Connecticut: Greenwood Press, 1984.

Getz, Irene Rose. "Moral Reasoning, Religion, and Attitudes Toward Human Rights." Doctoral dissertation, University of Minnesota, 1985.

Getz, Irene Rose. "The Relation of Moral and Religious Ideology to Human Rights." Unpublished manuscript. Minneapolis: University of Minnesota, n.d.

Gilligan, Carol. "In a Different Voice: Women's Conceptions of Self and of Morality." *Harvard Educational Review* 47 (1977), 481–517.

Goode, William J. "Librarianship from Occupation to Profession." *Library Quarterly* 31 (October, 1961), 316–318.

Hay, James. "A Study of Principled Moral Reasoning Within a Sample of Conscientious Objectors." *Moral Education Forum* 7 (1982), 1–8.

Hentoff, Nat. *First Freedom: The Tumultuous History of Free Speech in America.* New York: Delacorte, 1980.

Hopkins, Diane. "Censorship of School Library Materials and Its Implications." In *School Library Media Annual 1984,* Vol 2. Aaron, Shirley, and Pat Scales, eds. Littleton, Colorado: Libraries Unlimited, 1984, 9–22.

Jenkinson, Edward. *Censors in the Classroom: The Mind Benders.* Carbondale: Southern Illinois University Press, 1979.

Kohlberg, Lawrence. "Foreword." Rest, James R. *Development in Judging Moral Issues.* Minneapolis: University of Minnesota Press, 1979, vii-xvi.

Kohlberg, Lawrence. "From Is to Ought: How to Commit the Naturalistic Fallacy and Get Away with It in the Study of Moral Development." In Mischel, T., ed. *Cognitive Development and Epistemology.* New York: Academic Press, 1971, 151–236.

Kohlberg, Lawrence. *The Psychology of Moral Development,* Vol. 2: *Essays on Moral Development.* San Francisco: Harper and Row, 1984.

Kohlberg, Lawrence, and Daniel Candee. "The Relationship of Moral Judgment to Moral Action." In Kohlberg, Lawrence. *The Psychology of Moral Development.* San Francisco: Harper and Row, 1984, 498–581.

Kohlberg, Lawrence, and Richard H. Hersh. "Moral Development: A Review of the Theory." *Theory into Practice* 16 (1977), 53–59.

Kohlberg, Lawrence, and Clark Power. "Moral Development, Religious Thinking, and the Question of a Seventh Stage." *Zygon* 16 (1981), 203–259.

Lawrence, Jeanette Alice. "The Component Procedures of Moral Judgment Making." Doctoral dissertation, University of Minnesota, 1978.

Leedy, Paul D. *Practical Research: Planning and Design.* 3d ed. New York: Macmillan, 1985, 156.

Lemon, Nigel. *Attitudes and Their Measurement.* New York: John Wiley, 1973.

McDonald, Fran. *A Report of a Survey on Censorship in Public Elementary and High School Libraries and Public Libraries in Minnesota.* Minneapolis: Minnesota Civil Liberties Union, 1983.

McGeorge, Colin. "Some Correlates of Principled Moral Thinking in Young Adults." *Journal of Moral Education* 5 (1976), 265–273.

National Coalition Against Censorship. "Books on Trial: A Survey of Recent Cases." New York: National Coalition Against Censorship, 1985.

National Commission on Libraries and Information Science. "Censorship Activities in Public and Public School Libraries, 1975–1985." A Report to the Senate Subcommittee on Appropriations for the Departments of Labor, Health and Human Services, and Education and Related Agencies. U.S. National Commission on Libraries and Information Science. March, 1986.

O'Connor, Robert E. "Parental Sources and Political Consequences of Levels of Moral Reasoning Among European University Students." In Wilson, Richard W., and Gordon J. Schochet. *Moral Development and Politics.* New York: Praeger, 1980, 237–255.

O'Neil, Robert M. *Classrooms in the Crossfire: The Rights of Students, Parents, Teachers, Administrators, Librarians and the Community.* Bloomington: Indiana University Press, 1981.

Perritt, Patsy H. "School Library Media Certificate Requirements: 1988 Update—Part I." *School Library Journal* 34 (June-July, 1988), 31–38.

Pope, Michael. *Sex and the Undecided Librarian: A Study of Librarians' Opinions on Sexually Oriented Literature.* Metuchen, New Jersey: Scarecrow Press, 1974.

Reid, Herbert G., and Ernest J. Yanarella. "The Tyranny of the Categorical: On Kohlberg and the Politics of Moral Development." In Wilson, Richard W., and Gordon Schochet. *Moral Development and Politics.* New York: Praeger, 1980, 107–132.

Rest, James R. *Development in Judging Moral Issues.* Minneapolis: University of Minnesota Press, 1979.

Rest, James R. *Moral Development: Advances in Research and Theory.* New York: Praeger, 1986.

Rest, James R. "Morality." In Flavell, J., and E. Markman, eds. *Cognitive Development,* Vol. 4: *Manual of Child Psychology.* Mussen P., ed. New York: Wiley, 1982, 556–629.

Rest, James R. "A Psychologist Looks at the Teaching of Ethics." *Hastings Center Report* (February, 1982), 29–36.

Rest, James R. "Recent Research on an Objective Test of Moral Judgement: How the Important Issues of a Moral Dilemma Are Defined." In DePalma, David J., and Jeanne M. Foley. *Moral Development: Current Theory and Research.* Hillsdale, New Jersey: Lawrence Erlbaum, 1975, 75–93.

Rest, James R. *Revised Manual for the Defining Issues Test.* Minneapolis: Minnesota Moral Research Projects, 1979.

Rest, James R., Mark L. Davison, and Steven Robbins. "Age Trends in Judging Moral Issues: A Review of Cross-sectional, Longitudinal, and Sequential Studies of the Defining Issues Test." *Child Development* 49 (1978), 263–279.

Rest, James, Deborah Deemer, et al. "Life Experiences and Developmental Pathways." In Rest, James R. *Moral Development: Advances in Research and Theory.* New York: Praeger, 1986, 28–58.

Rest, James R., and Stephen J. Thoma. "Relation of Moral Judgment Development to Formal Education." *Developmental Psychology* 21 (1985), 709–714.

Serebnick, Judith. "An Analysis of the Relationship Between Book Reviews and the Inclusion of Potentially Controversial Books in Public Libraries." *Collection Building* 1 (1979), 8–53.

Serebnick, Judith. "Book Reviews and the Selection of Potentially Controversial Books in Public Libraries." *Library Quarterly* 51 (October, 1981), 390–409.

Serebnick, Judith. "Self-Censorship by Librarians: An Analysis of Checklist-Based Research." *Drexel Library Quarterly* 18 (Winter, 1982), 35–56.

Shaver, Darrel G. "A Longitudinal Investigation of the Moral Development of Selected Students at a Conservative Religious College." Doctoral dissertation, University of Iowa, 1984.

Shweder, Richard A., Eliot Turiel, and Nancy C. Much. "The Moral Intuitions of the Child," In Flavell, John H., and Lee Ross. *Social Cognitive Development: Frontiers and Possible Futures.* Cambridge: Cambridge University Press, 1981, 288–305.

Spence, Larry D. "Moral Judgment and Bureaucracy," In Wilson, Richard W., and Gordon J. Schochet. *Moral Development and Politics.* New York: Praeger, 1980, 137–171.

Sullivan, E. V. "A Study of Kohlberg's Structural Theory of Moral Development: A Critique of Liberal Social Science Ideology." *Human Development* 20 (1977), 352–376.

Thoma, Stephen J. "Estimating Gender Differences in the Comprehension and Preference of Moral Issues." Unpublished manuscript. Minneapolis: University of Minnesota, 1985.

Thomas, Cal. *Book Burning.* Westchester, Illinois: Crossways Books, Good News Publishers, 1983.

Watson, Jerry J., and Bill C. Snider. "Book Selection Pressures on School Library Media Specialists and Teachers." *School Media Quarterly* 9 (Winter, 1981), 95–101.

Woods, L. B. *A Decade of Censorship in America: The Threat to Classroom and Libraries.* Metuchen, New Jersey: Scarecrow Press, 1979.

Woods, L. B., and Lucy Salvatore. "Self-Censorship in Collection Development by High School Library Media Specialists." *School Media Quarterly* 9 (Winter, 1981), 102–108.

Woodworth, Mary. *Intellectual Freedom, the Young Adult, and Schools: A Wisconsin Study.* Madison: University of Wisconsin, 1976.

INDEX

ABOUT THE AUTHOR

FRANCES BECK MCDONALD (B.A., College of St. Scholastica; M.S. Mankato State University; Ph.D., University of Minnesota) is a professor in the Library Media Education Department at Mankato State University, Minnesota. She is the director of the Center for Children's and Young Adult Books, a selection and examination center at Mankato State University. Dr. McDonald is active in state and national library associations, having served as chair of the Young Adult Library Services Association Intellectual Freedom Committee and the American Association of School Librarians Intellectual Freedom Committee. She has served on the American Library Association Intellectual Freedom Committee and as chair of the Intellectual Freedom Round Table of the American Library Association. In 1990, Dr. McDonald began a second round as president of the Minnesota Coalition Against Censorship, having served in that position previously from 1979–1984. She was the 1992–1993 president of the Minnesota Educational Media Organization (MEMO) and previously chaired the MEMO Intellectual Freedom Committee and the MEMO *Information Power* Guidelines Implementation Committee.

Dr. McDonald is a frequent speaker at national and state library and media organizations on censorship and intellectual freedom issues and regularly conducts workshops on selection policy development and intellectual freedom. She edited the Minnesota Coalition Against Censorship publication, *Selection Policy Workbook* (distributed by the Minnesota Educational Media Organization, 1991) and has published many articles about intellectual freedom and censorship.